# CREATIVE
# TAPE
# RECORDING

# CREATIVE
# TAPE
# RECORDING

### VIVIAN CAPEL

FOUNTAIN PRESS: LONDON

Fountain Press,
M.A.P. Book Division,
Station Road,
Kings Langley,
Herts.


First Published 1972

ISBN 0 852 42106 0

Set and printed in England by Offset Litho at
Page Bros (Norwich) Ltd.

# CONTENTS

# PREFACE

MANY PEOPLE REGARD the tape recorder as an instrument for recording their favourite music or radio programme, baby's first gurgles and other family events. It is often treated like the family camera, a device for taking sound snap-shots as they occur or for copying the works of others. With the growing popularity of pre-recorded music tapes, especially cassettes, the recorder is used also to supplement the record-player.

These are all legitimate uses, but they are seldom *creative*. The use of a recorder to practice pronunciation when learning a language may be considered by some to be creative; yet although the purpose may be constructive, the end product is not the recording, which may later be erased, but the ability to speak the language. So once again it is not an example of creative tape recording.

Creative tape recording can be compared with painting. The canvas is the tape; the brushes, the recorder; the paints, the actual sounds. All are combined to produce the final result, but the skill and creative ability of the artist is the supreme factor. To make a copy of another painting is skilful but not creative. Few painters would be satisfied just making copies.

So it is with recording. The real satisfaction and sense of achievement comes with the making of creative, original recordings, which correspond with the artist's original finished paintings. They are complete and an end in themselves, work which can give pleasure on countless future occasions, and a permanent record of the skill and artistry of the maker. Tape recorder owners who limit their activities to the more mundane uses deprive themselves of a great deal of pleasure and satisfaction, for creative tape recording can be a very rewarding hobby.

Although skill is necessary to produce the finished work, the beginner should not let this put him off, for skill can be acquired with practice and guidance. Imaginative ideas are a vital requirement and these are not the sole prerogative of the veteran; beginners often have the knack of producing interesting and novel ideas. Imagination cannot be taught, of course, but the suggestions and examples in this book will provide some idea of what can be done and should stimulate original projects and approaches.

A deep technical knowledge is not necessary, any more than the artist needs to know the chemical formulae and reactions involved in manufacturing his paints and pigments. However, a grounding in basic principles is useful in order to get the best from one's equipment, and this is dealt with in the opening chapters, following which the techniques of tape recording are covered. The bulk of the book explores the various aspects of creative tape recording itself.

*Bristol 1972*                                   VIVIAN CAPEL

# CHAPTER ONE

# THE NATURE OF SOUND

THE WHOLE OBJECT OF RECORDING is to capture sounds for future hearings. Just as the artist needs to know about light and shade, the recordist needs to know the nature of sound, what it is, how sounds differ from each other, what happens when they travel through air and how they affect the microphone.

Basically, sound is a series of vibrations. It is produced by objects that are set into vibration, such as vocal chords in the human voice, the strings or reeds in musical instruments, the glass in chinking milk bottles. A high rate of vibration produces a high-pitched sound and a low rate a low pitch. Each vibration (the excursion of the object first to one side and then the other of its static or rest position) is termed a *cycle*, and the rate of vibration, hence the pitch, can be described as of so many cycles-per-second and is known as the *frequency*.

This is now usually expressed by the *Hertz*, which is a unit of one cycle-per-second and is abbreviated Hz, but the cycles-per-second designation is still sometimes encountered, with its abbreviation c/s. The lowest note on the piano is about 27Hz and the highest about 4kHz (4,000Hz) and the range of human audibility is generally considered to be from 16Hz to 16kHz but for many people, especially older ones, the upper limit may be much lower.

If a pure tone is being generated, the vibrating object moves rather like a piston in a car engine, smoothly, with the maximum speed occuring in the centre of its travel, slowing down at the ends until it stops momentarily to begin the reverse movement. If we make a graph of the motion it would appear as in Fig. 1.1; this is a complete cycle and is described as a *sinewave*.

## Harmonics

A pure tone is rarely encountered. It can be produced by a whistle, and by a flute played in its higher registers. Usually, the motion is more

1

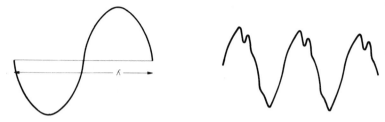

Fig. 1.1 (left) One complete cycle of a sinewave. The wavelength is the distance from the beginning to the end of one cycle.

Fig. 1.2 (right) The waveform generated by a piano note is of a complex nature.

complex, and a graph of the movement would be more like that of Fig. 1.2. Musical sounds contain frequencies that are multiples of the basic frequency (the fundamental). These are termed the second, third, fourth harmonic etc., and some sounds have up to twenty or more in varying proportions, in addition to the *fundamental*. Many sounds of a non-musical nature have a large proportion of other frequencies that are not exact multiples of the original (i.e., they are not *harmonically related*).

It is these additional frequencies that give a sound its character, that make one sound different from another even though it may have the same pitch or fundamental frequency. Thus a note played on a piano sounds very different from one of the same pitch played on the violin. Other factors contribute to the character of a sound; the way it starts, suddenly as with a snapping twig, or gradually as with the hoot of an owl; also the way the sound decays or dies away.

**Sound propagation**

How are sound vibrations transmitted through the air to become sound-waves? Air, being light and unstable, is readily disturbed or set in motion by the movement of any physical object. These motions affect adjacent air molecules which affect in turn those adjacent to them, and so the sound wave travels outward from its source. In still air of even temperature, the sound travels out in all directions to an equal degree, like ripples on a pond travelling out from a source of disturbance, but in air it travels in three dimensions instead of two.

Any shielding by nearby objects (or even the sound source itself) may modify the propagation pattern so that it is restricted to certain directions. Thus, with the human voice, sound intensity is greatest in the direction that the lips are facing. Air movements and temperature differences can also affect the way sound travels.

Although the ripples-on-the-pond illustration helps to describe the way sound travels outward from its source, it is misleading to think of it as consisting of up-and-down motions like sea waves. Rather, it follows a push-and-pull motion, creating local areas in the air of alternate compression and expansion. The sound wave is rather like a jolt passing along a train of goods trucks. Fig. 1.3 shows the general principle.

As the speed of sound in air is constant at any one temperature, high-frequency sounds will have their waves closer together than low-frequency ones. We can perhaps get a better idea of this by imagining sea waves; those that arrive in quick succession are spaced more closely than those that take longer. Thus it can be seen that the distance from the start of one wave to the next (the wavelength, represented by the Greek letter $\lambda$) is inversely proportional to the frequency, so that a high frequency means a short wavelength. The relationship between the two, with actual figures, is shown in Table 1.1, and is useful when designing or calculating the acoustic properties of rooms or studios.

When travelling out from the source, energy is lost by the sound waves and turned into heat; hence the intensity (amplitude) decreases with distance until it is swamped by the general or ambient noise level of the surroundings, or it is too weak to be detected. This is an important factor to remember when considering microphone placings relative to the sound source. A distant position may pick up the sound well enough to be amplified, but there may be a high level of ambient noise to detract from or even obscure the wanted sound.

## Reverberation

Outdoors, the sound travels outward and is lost unless it is reflected from some distant objects, in which case it can return seconds later to

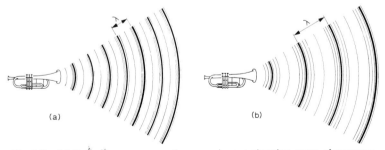

Fig. 1.3   (a) Sound source generating sound wave showing areas of compression and expansion. As it is of a high frequency the areas are close together and the wavelength (indicated) is short. (b) a low frequency note with longer wavelength.

give an echo. Echos are obtained from large hard reflective areas at right-angles to the direction of sound travel. Large walls and cliffs are the most usual sources.

Indoors, sound is reflected from a multitude of surfaces—walls, ceiling, floor, windows and furniture. These reflections are re-reflected about the room until they are either absorbed by sound-absorbent surfaces or they eventually die away. The effect is known as *reverberation* and a specific reverberation time can be quoted for a given room or studio. This is the time taken for the sound to die away to a millionth of its original intensity. For the average living room reverberation times of about half-a-second are common.

Much depends on the size of the room, but mostly it is the furnishings that influence the acoustics. The difference in reverberation between an empty room and a furnished one is very marked and this can be noticed by the sound of the voice in a room that has been stripped for decorating. Soft furnishings absorb sound, especially the high frequencies, so a room that is curtained and carpeted, and contains upholstered chairs, will have little reverberation and will reduce the high frequencies. Recordings made in such rooms sound muffled and dead, while those made in a sparsely furnished room with a wood or lino floor sound bright and clear. Those made in the open air do not usually sound muffled because there is nothing to absorb the high frequencies, but they sound dead because of the lack of reverberation.

Some places are highly reverberent; swimming-baths, for example, and to a lesser extent the domestic bathroom. This is because of the presence of tiling and glazed surfaces, which are highly reflective to sound. This can cause lack of clarity because sounds tend to run into each other. Music and singing sounds better with a degree of reverberation, which is why many people with poor voices sound quite reasonable in the bath!

**Resonance**

That acoustics have a profound effect on recordings, is often not recognised by amateurs. These various acoustic conditions, though, can be put to good use and various effects can be obtained by choosing the place of recording.

All physical objects have a natural frequency at which they will vibrate more readily than at any other. This is known as the *resonant frequency* and the condition is termed *resonance*. It is determined by the mass and the size of the object. The principle is exploited with musical instruments where the natural resonance of strings and air columns is altered by varying their lengths and so producing notes of

| Wavelength (ft) | Frequency (Hz) | Wavelength (in.) | Frequency (Hz) |
|---|---|---|---|
| 50 | 22·5 | 12 | 1,125 |
| 40 | 28 | 10 | 1,300 |
| 20 | 56 | 8 | 1,700 |
| 15 | 75 | 6 | 2,250 |
| 10 | 112 | 4 | 3,400 |
| 5 | 225 | 2 | 6,750 |
| 2·5 | 450 | 1 | 13,500 |
| 2 | 562 | | |

Table 1.1    Wavelength–Frequency Relationship.

different frequencies. Although resonance is necessary in the *production* of music and almost any natural sound, it can be a nuisance in the recording and *reproduction* of sounds. Moving parts in microphones and loudspeakers have their own natural resonances, and these cause the particular frequencies in the reproduced sound to be over-emphasised. Thus the result is not a faithful copy of the original.

Fortunately, modern sound and recording equipment of good quality is designed to minimise the effects so that to the ear there appears to be little difference between original and reproduced sound due to over-emphasis of certain frequencies as a result of resonance. It is often found in cheaper equipment, though, particularly with microphones, as we shall see in the next chapter.

**Room Resonance**

A room or studio is in effect an enclosed container of air, and so the air will exhibit resonance effects. There are three main resonances, each corresponding to one of three room dimensions; the length, width and height. These dimensions will excite resonance at the frequency which equals half its wavelength. For example, the wavelength of a 56Hz tone is about 20 feet. A room dimension of 10 feet (half the wavelength) will therefore produce a resonance at 56Hz. There will also be lesser secondary resonances at frequencies corresponding to a quarter wavelength.

The sound pressure in a room at a primary resonant frequency will be much larger than it would be at a non-resonant frequency. If two of the room dimensions are the same, in other words if the room is square, then the resonant frequency will be reinforced and increased in effect. Having all three dimensions the same, or a cube shape, is even worse.

In order to spread the resonances evenly, the ideal room for the purposes of sound reproduction should have the ratio of 1·25 times and 1·6 times the smallest dimension. It will be noticed that room resonances affect only the lowest audio frequencies; these can be important when reproducing music with equipment that has an extended bass response, but the average tape recorder does not have a good enough bass response to raise room resonance problems.

The ratio given above applies to small rooms. For modern domestic rooms of medium size, the ratio of 1:1·6:2·5 is acceptable. For large rooms, small halls etc., a ratio of 1:1·25:3·2 is acceptable.

Human speech and the majority of sounds other than music do not have strong low frequencies around the values of room resonances. So, with recording, they are not likely to be troublesome. It is the reverberation and high-frequency absorption characteristic of a room that is going to have the greatest effect on a recording.

## Dynamic Range

The relationship between very loud and very soft sounds is called the *dynamic range*. With human hearing, this is wide; a whisper and the tick of a watch can be heard, as can the roar of a motor-cycle or a jet plane. The range approaches 20,000,000 times from quietest to loudest. In sound-pressure ratios, this represents 4250:1, or around 72·5dB (see below). Normal concert range is around 60dB.

With the loudest sounds, the linkage in the ar between the eardrum and the inner ear changes its pivotal positions so that sound impact is reduced, while the quiet sounds are transmitted through the ear with the maximum of efficiency. It is this marvellous 'design feature' that gives our ears such a wide dynamic range, and at the same time provides a measure of protection from damage to the inner ear by very loud sounds. There are, of course, limits, and over a certain level loud noise will produce permanent damage to the ear.

It is very difficult for recording equipment to handle a large dynamic range; certainly at present even the most expensive tape recorders cannot compete with the human ear. Very quiet sounds tend to get lost in background noise due to effects in the tape and the valves or transistors. In order to preserve a signal-to-noise ratio (the 'signal' refers to the electrical equivalent to the sound in the amplifying circuits) so that the noise is not very obtrusive, the sound cannot be allowed to fall below a certain minimum level.

On the other hand, high volume levels will overload the microphones, amplifying stages and tape, so these must be kept below a certain maximum amount, otherwise distortion will result. Thus, there is a minimum and maximum level outside of which recording cannot successfully be made. Some recorders have an automatic-volume-level control which reduces the louder sounds and prevents overloading. It also restricts the dynamic range.

## Logarithmic Law

One further interesting fact about sound, or rather the ear's reaction to it, is that differences in both pitch and intensity follow a logarithmic or square law. We have already referred to the fact that increasingly louder sounds have a progressively smaller effect on the ear. The effect is reflected in the decibel notation used to compare relative levels of signals. One decibel (dB) is the smallest difference between one sound and a louder one that can be detected with the ear.

The decibel is not an absolute unit of sound as it is often considered to be, but expresses a *ratio* between two sounds or signals. Some common values are: 6dB = 2 times; 10dB = 3 times; 20dB = 10 times; 30dB = 30 times (an easy one to remember); 40dB = 100 times, and 60dB = 1,000 times. Notice how ratios can be simply worked out by just adding the dB, thus $3 \times 10 = 30$ times becomes 10dB + 20dB = 30dB.

The effects of frequency are similar. If we had a tone of 1kHz and then doubled it to 2kHz, and then to 4kHz and 8kHz, the differences would sound the same even though to start with it would be a difference of 1kHz, and the last one would be 4kHz. Musicians call these differences *octaves* because they are based on an eight-note musical scale. So a note that is an octave higher than another is double its frequency irrespective of what that frequency actually is.

CHAPTER TWO

# MICROPHONES

---

IT IS BY MEANS OF THE MICROPHONE that the sound picture is 'seen'. There are several different types and each of these can be designed to possess different characteristics. Some are most suitable for one purpose, and others for different ones. A knowledge of microphones and application of that knowledge is a big step towards successful recording.

**Crystal Microphones**

One of the most common microphones is the crystal type. Certain crystalline materials, some occuring in the natural state (such as rochelle salt) and others man-made (such as barium titanate and lead zirconate) exhibit the *piezo-electric* effect. If any of these are subjected to pressure or strain, an electrical voltage will be generated proportional to the amount of pressure. In the microphone, a thin slice of the crystal is secured at one end and a light aluminium cone brought to bear on the other. Sound waves make the cone vibrate to-and-fro, and so pressures are exerted on the crystal in sympathy with the sound waves. This in turn generates corresponding electrical voltage impulses.

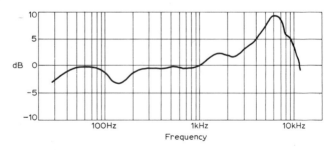

Fig. 2.1   Frequency response curve of a typical crystal microphone. Note the peak at around 5kHz.

8

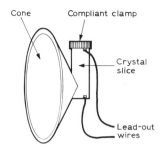

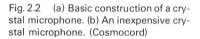

Fig. 2.2 (a) Basic construction of a crystal microphone. (b) An inexpensive crystal microphone. (Cosmocord)

The frequency response of crystal microphones does not extend much above about 10kHz. This is adequate for speech, but music and sounds containing a high order of harmonics sound rather dull when the higher frequencies are thus curtailed. Of course, if the recorder itself has a limited high-frequency response, there is little point in worrying about the response of the microphone.

Generally, crystal microphones do not respond equally to all frequencies within their range. Minor variations make little audible difference, but the more pronounced ones give the microphone a characteristic 'tone' so that if the microphone was changed during a recording, the difference in tone would be noticeable. A microphone should faithfully convey to the recorder only what it 'hears', and this requires an instrument with the 'flat' frequency response possessed only by the more expensive types.

## Cone Resonance

In the crystal microphone, the natural resonance of the cone and the crystal produce a peak in the response curve as shown in Fig. 2.1. This emphasis of frequencies around 5kHz can give an artificial brightness which partially compensates for the lack of higher frequencies, but it can also result in a hard tone. String music sounds harsh and scratchy, and voices that tend to lisp or sound sibilant, have the effect accentuated.

Background noise tends to be concentrated around 5kHz and just below. This is because the extreme low and high frequencies of ambient sounds become absorbed and attenuated, leaving the band of middle-frequencies predominant. A microphone with a peak around this frequency will be particularly sensitive to such background noise.

However, this will be an advantage if surrounding noises are required to give atmosphere, such as with on-the-spot recordings at various locations. For this reason, some microphone manufacturers describe the peak as a 'presence effect', cunningly making a drawback appear to be an advantage!

Another factor which must be considered with the crystal microphone is that the crystal itself is fragile and can easily be fractured if subjected to mechanical shock. Also, the natural crystals are adversely affected by heat and humidity, although the man-made ones are rather more stable in this respect.

Crystals are *high-impedance* devices, that is they generate a relatively high voltage and low current. It is essential that the input of the recorder is also high-impedance, otherwise there will be a loss of low frequencies and generally low sensitivity. A minimum impedance of 1 megohm is usually required to match a crystal microphone. Incidentally, with all microphones the impedance must match that of the recorder input circuits within the limits, generally, of 1 : 10. Note that the stated impedance in a specification may actually be an 'acceptance' figure; i.e., stated input impedance of $1k\Omega$ may refer to a *measured* input impedance of $10\Omega$ (see later).

## Moving Coil Microphones

A light aluminium cone is fitted with a small cylinder at its apex. On this is wound a coil of wire supported in the gap between the poles of a powerful magnet. One of the poles passes up inside the cylinder and the other encloses it from the outside. Thus a strong magnetic field passes through the windings of the coil. Since the outer edge of the cone is supported by a flexible material to the frame of the instrument, when sound waves reach it the cone moves backwards and forwards through the static magnetic field (see Fig. 2.3).

When an electrical conductor such as a wire moves through a magnetic field, a voltage is induced in it, and when the wire is coiled up so that a number of its turns pass through the field, the voltage is multiplied by the number of the turns. Thus, motion which is in sympathy with the incoming sound wave produces a similar electric current. A moving coil loudspeaker operates on the same principle and the construction is very similar, but it is electric current which is converted into motion instead of the reverse.

The cone movement is freer and the action more refined than the crystal, so the frequency response is generally smoother and extends much higher. However, there is still cone resonance at around 5kHz, although some of the more expensive instruments succeed in reducing the peak, without eliminating it entirely.

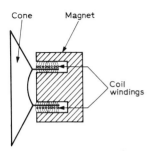

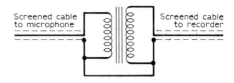

Fig. 2.4 (right) Theoretical circuit of microphone transformer.

Fig. 2.3 (left) Basic construction of a moving coil microphone.

What has been said about the tone colour of crystal microphones, background noise and presence effect, also applies to the moving-coil instrument. However, moving-coil microphones are very sturdy and will stand a considerable amount of rough treatment, being particularly suited for on-location recording. Temperature and humidity will not unduly affect them, although they should not be directly exposed to water such as by leaving them out in the rain without protection.

## Low Impedance

The moving-coil microphone is a low-impedance instrument so it cannot be used directly with a valved tape recorder, which requires a high-impedance type, or a transistor recorder which often needs a medium impedance. The impedance must be changed from low to medium or from low to high by means of a matching microphone-transformer. Some microphones incorporate an inbuilt transformer. Owners of valve recorders who wish to improve on the crystal microphone supplied with the instrument will find such a microphone the best and most convenient for general use.

Some moving-coil microphones that incorporate a transformer include an arrangement for selecting either high, low or medium impedance. For the purposes of microphone matching, medium impedance is anything from 200 to 600 ohms and low impedance is 30 to 50 ohms. High impedance is around 1 megohm (a million ohms) for crystal units, down to 47,000 ohms for transformer-matched moving-coils. It can be seen that the term high-impedance covers a wide range.

The medium-impedance setting is usually best for transistor tape recorders, but the high can also be used because the 'high' of a moving-coil transformer microphone is much less than that of the crystal, which should not be used with transistors. Some recent tape-recorders employ *field-effect transistors* (FET). These have high-impedance inputs and so high-impedance microphones should be used with them, even crystals being permissible. The maker's instruction booklet should give information such as the impedance of the input circuits, since input circuits nowadays can often accomodate 30Ω microphones quite effectively.

A low-impedance moving-coil microphone, i.e., one without an internal transformer, can be converted to either medium or high-impedance by using an external transformer. Expensive tape recorders may have inbuilt transformers and so can accept low-impedance inputs directly, but this is rare. Normally, the transformer will have to be inserted into the connecting cable.

The transformer consists of two coils of wire or windings, wound on a laminated iron core which increases the magnetic coupling between them. It is drawn in a circuit diagram as shown in Fig. 2.4.

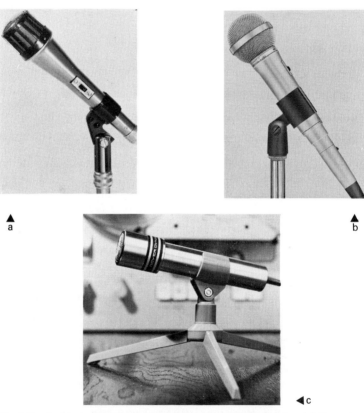

▲
a

▲
b

◀c

Fig. 2.5   A group of moving coil microphones in various styles. (a) Grampian GC2, (b) Turner 700, (c) Beyer M550LM.

## Hum and Screening

Screened wire is always used for the microphone cable and consists of a single insulated stranded wire covered with stranded metal braiding. This braiding (screening) serves as the second wire and it is earthed by being connected to the chassis or metal work of the recorder. Ordinary twin flex would pick up hum from nearby electricity mains wiring and, although the amount would be small, it would be fully amplified along with the signal from the microphone. The screening shields the inner conductor from any such hum fields, which are harmlessly directed to earth along it.

The same thing applies to any microphone transformer which may be inserted in the cable. This is far more likely to pick up hum than the cable because the windings are designed to be magnetically sensitive to each other and therefore will be sensitive to external magnetic hum-fields. The transformer and its connections must therefore be well screened by means of a metal casing.

If strong hum-fields are present, even the ordinary metal shielding around the transformer will not give complete protection. For this reason a special metal (*mu-metal*) is sometimes used to shield the transformer and gives almost 100% protection. This metal is very expensive, and can triple the price of the transformer.

Obviously, then, the microphone with the built-in transformer will be the most economical, costing not much more than transformerless models. Furthermore it avoids the inconvenience of having the transformer dangling in the lead, although there are times when an external transformer could be an advantage.

## Cable Losses

Screened lead used for microphone cables has a high capacitance between the inner conductor and the braiding. As this is proportional to its length, a long run of cable has a very high capacitance compared to ordinary twin flex. This capacitance affects the circuit to a degree depending on the impedance of the circuit. For high-impedance circuits, it will mean a loss of the high frequencies (as if a capacitor were connected directly across the input socket) but for medium and low impedances the loss becomes negligible.

With three or four yards of cable, the cable losses can be ignored and a high-impedance arrangement is quite satisfactory, but when the cable length exceeds about 10 yards, then high-frequency loss begins to occur within the frequency range of the recorder. Longer runs will have a more marked effect. For the inexpensive recorders operating at low speeds the effect will not be significant because the high frequencies of that order will not be recorded anyway, but for better machines that run at faster speeds the losses would degrade the quality.

For cable lengths much in excess of 10 yards, then, low or medium-impedance operation should be adopted. As transistor recorders are usually supplied with moving-coil microphones of medium-impedance, the cable lengths can be extended considerably without ill-effect. It is not possible to use a transformer with a crystal microphone to reduce its effective impedance, which is high, so this type of microphone should never be used with a long lead. In fact, the high-frequency losses are greater with these microphones than with the moving-coil high impedance type, and the cable length should never exceed 6 yards.

Where an extended microphone cable is needed for use with a valve recorder, a low or medium-impedance microphone should be used with an external transformer. Always fit the transformer at the recorder end of the cable and not near the microphone, otherwise the cable between it and the recorder will be operating at high-impedance and one might just as well have a high-impedance microphone. When connected near the recorder, the greatest part of the cable between it and the microphone will be at low-impedance, which is what we want to eliminate losses.

**Microphone Transformers**

Microphone transformers are obtainable in two styles: chassis-mounting and in-line. The former is mounted on an amplifier or recorder chassis, the connections being made to the input socket thus converting it to accept low- or medium-impedance microphones. If low-impedance microphones are to be used exclusively, this is the most convenient type to use as there will be no transformer getting in the way on the lead. Chassis-mounting types are fitted by means of a metal clip or a screwed bush and the connections are made by free insulated wires that are brought out through a hole in the screening.

The in-line transformer usually has a short length of screened lead already fitted to one end, so that a microphone plug can be fitted directly to it. Terminals are provided at the other end which are covered by a screened cap so that the lead from the microphone can be connected in.

**Ribbon Microphones**

The ribbon microphone works on the same electro-magnetic principle as the moving-coil, but the construction is quite different. A thin corrugated ribbon, usually of aluminium foil, is stretched edgeways

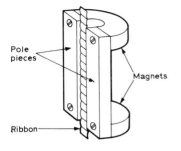

Fig. 2.6 Basic construction of a ribbon microphone.

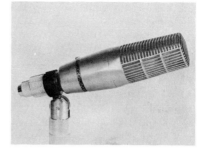

Fig. 2.7 A representative ribbon microphone (Melodium).

between the pole pieces of a powerful magnet. So that there will be maximum concentration of magnetic lines of force through the ribbon, the poles are very close to the ribbon and the clearance a matter of a few thousandths of an inch (see Fig. 2.6).

The microphone is open at the back as well as the front, and sound waves pass right through, around the ribbon. The velocity of the waves as they pass cause the ribbon to move backwards and forwards, and for this reason the ribbon microphone is sometimes referred to as a *velocity* type. The crystal and moving-coil microphones, because they are operated by the pressure of the sound waves on the diaphragm, are often described as *pressure* microphones.

Electrically, the ribbon microphone is like a moving-coil microphone with just a single turn of wire, because the movement of the ribbon within the magnetic field generates the signal current, and the output connections are made at either end of the ribbon. The impedance is very low, just a fraction of an ohm, and the voltage generated is likewise low. All ribbon microphones must include a transformer even to bring them up to the normal low impedance of 30 ohms. Some models include transformers that bring them up to medium-impedance, and a few up to high-impedance.

## Low Ribbon Mass

The mass of the ribbon is far less than that of a cone or diaphragm with a coil mounted on it. Thus it responds well to sudden sounds or transients, and is also capable of moving very rapidly to react to high frequencies. Hence the transient and high-frequency response is better than with moving-coil or crystal types.

The resonant frequency depends in part upon the mass of the

particular object, the lower the mass the higher the frequency. Hence the resonant frequency of the ribbon will be much higher than that of the cone and coil in the moving-coil microphone. In fact, the resonant peak will be higher than the top limit of the frequency range. Thus over its range, the ribbon microphone is substantially flat and free from peaks, and quality is much smoother and more natural sounding than either moving-coil or crystal types. There is no harshness in the treble, or emphasis on sibilants.

On a direct comparison, it might seem that the ribbon microphone is lacking in brilliance and clarity compared with the moving-coil. Careful listening, however, will detect the high frequencies, but the artificial brilliance of the moving-coil microphone makes the ribbon microphone *seem* deficient at the high frequency end of its range. Bass frequencies tend to be emphasised with ribbon microphones, but this helps to compensate for the lack of bass given by most tape recorder loudspeakers. The effect is most noticed when the microphone is held too close to the lips, and can be reduced by moving further away.

With ribbon microphones the explosive consonants 'P' and 'B' produce a loud noise on the recording if the microphone is held too close to the lips. This is due to the rapid violent rush of air when the lips separate, blowing the ribbon forward. Again this can be prevented by
not holding the microphone too close, or by speaking over the top of it rather than into it.

Although ribbon microphones give less output than the moving-coil, modern ones are quite sensitive, and if of the correct impedance, will give sufficient signal for most recorders.

## Disadvantages of Ribbons

Ribbon microphones are expensive. The cheapest can cost up to half the price of the recorder, and the more expensive can cost more than the recorder. This undoubtedly is a drawback for the amateur user, but while this top-grade microphone would be wasted with a modestly-priced tape recorder, for the serious amateur with good equipment it will be a good investment.

The other main disadvantage is fragility. Although not affected by heat and humidity as are crystal types, they can be damaged by mechanical shock. The ribbon has only a very small clearance to the magnet poles on either side, and a severe jolt can displace it and cause it to foul them.

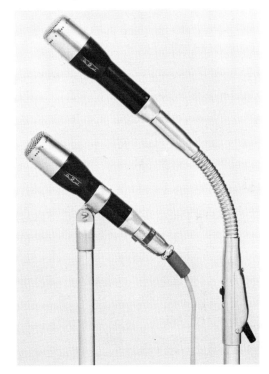

Fig. 2.8 Examples of modern capacitor microphones: Pearl HM49 (left) and Neumann KMS85i (right).

## Capacitor Microphones

It is unlikely that any but the professional users will invest in the conventional *capacitor* microphone. It consists of a capacitor of which one plate or electrode comprises a thin plastics diaphragm coated with metallising. Sound waves cause the diaphragm to vibrate and this varies the capacitance between it and the fixed member.

The diaphragm has no self-rigidity, but is kept taut by a polarising voltage applied between it and the other member. This, together with the extremely low mass, which is even less than a ribbon of metal foil, gives a very smooth frequency response and response to transients which excels even the ribbon. Special input circuits are required which, among other things, supply the necessary polarising voltage, and are very expensive. Only top-grade professional recorders would really do justice to the best capacitor microphones.

A later development of the capacitor microphone—the Electret—has a very thin polymer film diaphragm and an integrated circuit preamplifier built into its body. The compact design allows these to be sometimes mounted in the tape recorder itself.

## Microphone Presentation

Microphones can be housed in different ways, each having a particular purpose. The flat housing used for the inexpensive microphones supplied with most tape recorders can be hand-held, or a pivoted rest extended to enable them to stand vertically.

Another housing is the stick-type, which has a cylindrical or tapered handle with the actual microphone mounted at one end and the cable emerging from the other. It can be hand-held or slotted into a holder on a desk or floor stand. The stick type is sometimes supplied with tape recorders. A further housing is the stand-type. Here the microphone is contained in a case, usually of metal, with a screw connector at the base for fixing to a stand. These are used mainly for public address purposes.

## Built-in Switches

Some microphones, usually the stick-types, have built-in on/off switches. Although sometimes useful, it is easy to accidentally knock the switch to the off position when recording, ending with a partially blank tape! They tend also to be rather unreliable and make poor contact, resulting in crackling and loss of programme.

Fig. 2.9   Two microphones from the Eagle range. Left—model DD1 designed for use with cassette tape recorders and fitted with remote stop/start switch. Right—model UD76HL studio quality cardioid fitted with a music/speech contour control and a dual-impedance switched transformer.

In some portable battery recorders, the switch on the microphone will switch the *recorder* on and off. This 'remote' facility is useful, because the recorder can be set up and switched to record, then switched off at the microphone. A recording can then be started by

Fig. 2.10 A low cost directional microphone for amateurs unable to afford a studio quality model, the Beyer model M81ON dynamic cardioid.

operating the microphone switch. It is an ideal arrangement for interviews and on-the-spot recordings, where the recorder is carried in a shoulder-strap case.

It should be noted, however, that as the machine is then left in an 'engaged' position, there can be deformation of rubber tyres under pressure (pinch wheels and intermediate wheels). The practice, therefore, should be for short periods only, with the mechanism neutralised as soon as possible.

**Polar Response**

Microphones do not pick up sound equally from all directions, and some cut off quite sharply when turned away from the sound source. The angle of acceptance varies with different types and how they are used, and this can be put to good use in discriminating between wanted and unwanted sounds.

The response of a microphone to sounds coming from various directions, plotted on a circular graph, is a *polar diagram,* the concentric circles expressing sensitivity levels in decibels and the degrees around the circle the sound acceptance angle. Typical polar diagrams are shown in Fig. 2.11.

## Cardioid and Hypercardioids

Microphones using a cone (crystal and moving-coil) are most sensitive to sounds coming directly from the front. The response falls at the sides and drops to a minimum at the rear, where the body of the microphone shields the cone from incoming sounds. The polar diagram (broken line) is roughly heart-shaped, and for this reason the response is said to be *cardioid* (Fig. 2.11a).

Some microphones are physically designed to reduce the pick-up at the sides. The response shown at Fig. 2.11b is *hypercardioid* and is useful where there is a high level of unwanted noise in the surrounding area. The microphone can be directed at the wanted sound source, the unwanted sounds being reduced.

## Omnidirectional Response

An omnidirectional response is one equal in all directions, in practice limited by the shielding effect from the case and bodywork. However, this characteristic can be achieved with a cardioid instrument by mounting it vertically. The only area from which there will be minimal response will be downward (from the floor) so that for all practical purposes the response is omnidirectional. To avoid the less sensitive areas that are level with the sides and behind, the microphone should be placed on a lower plane that the sound sources. The sounds will thus be coming slightly forward of the sides where the sensitivity is a little greater.

A snag with a low level placing of the microphone is the possible shielding of incoming sounds by various objects. An alternative is to suspend the microphone above the area, pointing downwards, providing pickup all the way around and beneath it, but very little above it. This is especially advantageous when recording in a hall or building with an echoing roof, as the excess reverberations will be reduced.

It should be noted that the hypercardioid is not so good for use as an omnidirectional microphone in this manner, because the sensitivity at the sides is curtailed.

## Figure-Eight Response

Ribbon microphones are open at both front and rear, and accept sound equally from opposite directions. The sides, shielded by the magnetic pole pieces, and also because the ribbon is incapable of side-to-side movement, are the areas of minimum sensitivity. In fact, quite loud sounds from the sides will produce little response, an effect that can be

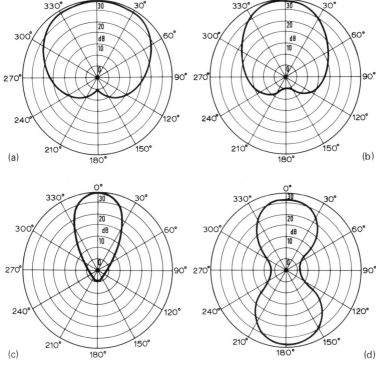

Fig. 2.11 Typical microphone polar diagrams. (a) top left—cardioid. (b) top right—hypercardioid. (c) bottom left—reflector type. (d) bottom right—figure-of-eight pattern.

quite useful. This response (Fig. 2.11d) is known as bi-directional, or more descriptively *figure-eight*.

While this is the natural response of the ribbon microphone some are constructed to give a cardioid or even hypercardioid response. These, too, can be very useful in certain circumstances. Other ribbon microphones are supplied with detachable pads that can be inserted or removed from the back. Thus the response can be tailored to requirements, either full figure-eight, or partially suppressed rear pickup.

## Ultra-directional Types

There is another type of polar response which can be obtained in either of two ways. This is the ultra-directional narrow-beam microphone, with a high forward-sensitivity but a large rejection at the sides and rear (see Fig. 2.11c). One method of achieving this is by the barrel or rifle type of microphone, where the actual microphone is placed at the bottom of a long tube which contains a bundle of tubes of different lengths, each effective at one particular frequency.

Alternatively, vents or holes are introduced along the side of a single tube which produce interference or cancellation effects at various frequencies. Both methods cause cancellation of sounds coming from the rear or the sides.

The other way of getting a high forward-sensitivity, and reducing side and rear sounds, is by using a reflector. This takes the form of a polished metal parabola two or more feet in diameter. The microphone is mounted a few inches away from the reflector and pointing into it at its centre. Sounds coming from the front fall on the reflector and are focused towards the microphone. Thus, relatively weak sounds falling on the large reflector area are concentrated to a high-intensity level at the microphone. Sounds not coming from exactly in front of the unit are reflected to a point away from the microphone (Fig. 2.12).

The barrel-type of microphone is generally more convenient to operate and transport and is frequently used by professional news recordists, in TV and film studios, and anywhere where distant sound sources are not easily accessible to ordinary microphones. They are rather expensive, and the microphone and the barrel are part of the

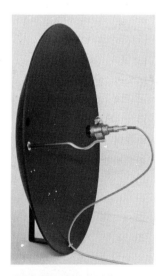

Fig. 2.12    For obtaining extreme directivity, a parabolic reflector can be used, such as the example shown by Grampian. The diagram on the right shows how the sound can be focused on to the microphone by the paraboloid.

same unit and so it cannot be detached for more conventional applications. These are serious disadvantages to the amateur, and so the reflector is a better proposition. Admittedly it is rather cumbersome to operate and carry about, but it is not expensive, and any stick microphone can be fitted and removed as required. Recording of bird songs is a common use for the reflector.

Both barrel and reflector types need careful aiming at the source if the maximum benefit is to be obtained from the ultra-directional characteristic. Some form of support or stand will in most cases be necessary so that the microphone can be kept trained on the source.

### Polar Response and Frequency

All the directional features of the microphones discussed hold good for only one frequency or a narrow band of frequencies. Many published polar-diagrams have several contours, each for a separate frequency.

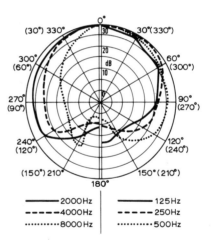

Fig. 2.13 A practical cardioid polar diagram plotted at the six frequencies shown in the key, three different frequencies being depicted on the left and right halves of the diagram.

| ——— 2000Hz | ——— 125Hz |
| – – – 4000Hz | – – – 250Hz |
| ·········· 8000Hz | ·········· 500Hz |

However, the differences are not great, and the widest divergence is at the extreme ends of the frequency spectrum. High frequencies are more directional than the lower ones and so pickup at the sides and back will be less than indicated in the illustrations.

In effect the pickup area will be narrower, so the cardioid will be more like a hypercardioid at high frequencies. Sound sources that contain high frequencies should not be placed too far off centre otherwise they will tend to sound dull and lifeless. On the other hand if some sources are over-endowed with high frequencies, such as a voice with pronounced sibilants, an off-centre placing could improve matters.

B

# CHAPTER THREE

# PRINCIPLES OF
# TAPE RECORDING

THE OUTPUT OF THE MICROPHONE is an electric current of varying intensity which corresponds with the air pressure variations of the original sound wave. This is applied via the microphone socket to successive stages of amplification by valves or transistors until it is magnified sufficiently to operate the recording head. A large electrical signal is not needed at the head itself, but is required in the stage feeding the head. This is because in order to obtain an even response to all applied frequencies, a very inefficient method of coupling the head to its driving stage must be used.

### Record-head and Tape

The recording head is made up of a coil of wire wound on a laminated ferrous yoke which concentrates the magnetic field produced by the current in the winding. A gap is deliberately made in the yoke to break the continuity of the magnetic circuit, so that the edges of the gap become pole-pieces of an electro-magnet, and when current is flowing

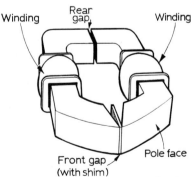

Fig. 3.1    Basic details of a recording head.

24

in the coil a small but intense magnetic field is produced around the gap. When signal currents are passed through the coil, a varying magnetic field appears at the gap in sympathy with the applied signal.

The recording tape consists of a narrow strip made of polyester, p.v.c. or acetate just under a quarter-of-an-inch wide in standard reel recorders and an eighth-of-an-inch wide in cassette recorders, coated with iron oxide which is deposited in the form of very fine particles. As it moves over the record head the magnetic field at the gap magnetises that section of the tape which is passing, the degree of magnetism on the tape depending on the strength of the field at that moment. Thus, all along the tape, we have varying magnetic patterns corresponding to the instantaneous values of the field in the gap.

**Magnetic Behaviour**

Fig. 3.1 shows a recorded track on a magnetic tape. The head-gap, being a vertical slit, produces vertical 'stripes' of magnetism; as the applied wave rises to a maximum in a positive direction, so a more intense magnetic area is produced on the tape. However, the amount of magnetism is not exactly proportional to the magnetising force, and conversely when demagnetising back through zero to build up in the opposite polarity again, the magnetic effect is disproportionate.

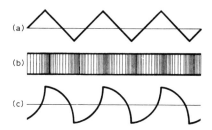

Fig. 3.2    If the sawtooth waveform (a) is applied as a magnetising force to a tape, the magnetic pattern would appear as at (b), giving a recorded wave as at (c). This is due to the non-linear manner in which magnetic materials accept magnetism from a magnetising force.

Fig. 3.2 shows a hypothetical signal current which rises and falls in a perfectly linear manner (this type of waveform would not occur with natural sounds and is used here for illustration only). If this were applied to a recording head, the magnetic pattern on the tape would be as in Fig. 3.2b and the recorded waveform as in Fig. 3.2c. It will be noticed that after an initial curved rise, the magnetism decays more slowly than the applied current and it reaches zero after the current has begun to rise in the opposite direction. It then rapidly rises in the opposite polarity and decays slowly. Any applied waveform, whatever its shape, would be seriously distorted as would be the reproduced sound.

## D.C. Bias

One solution is not to allow the magnetising force pass through a zero point, as it is the rise from and return to zero which creates the difficulty. If a steady fixed magnetising force is maintained by passing a d.c. current through the head, and the signal is superimposed on this, it will increase and decrease but never fall to zero. This is known as *d.c. bias* and is used in many cheap portable recorders because of its simplicity.

The amount of magnetism that a tape will accept, from zero to saturation, governs the amplitude or level of the signal that can be recorded on it. The d.c. bias system uses just one of the straight or linear parts of the magnetisation characteristic, thus the level of the recorded signal is low and so is the ratio of signal to background hiss.

## A.C. Bias

To overcome these deficiencies, *a.c. bias* is generally used. An oscillator generates a sinewave of many times the frequency of the highest signal-frequency to be recorded. The signals are superimposed on it by feeding both of them into the record-head together (See Fig. 3.3).

The initial magnetisation curve is fairly straight except for curves at the bottom and top. The d.c. bias system utilises this straight portion, avoiding the bottom curve by not passing through the zero

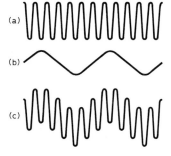

Fig. 3.3 (a) High frequency bias waveform, (b) applied signal, and (c) the result—a superimposed waveform.

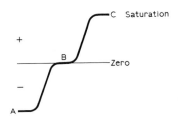

Fig. 3.4 The initial magnetising curve from zero to saturation (B–C). This can be extended in the opposite direction (B–A) with opposite polarity giving the combined characteristic A—C.

point, and the top one by not approaching the saturation level. This initial curve holds good for magnetisation in both positive and negative directions, so we can draw it end-to-end as in Fig. 3.4.

Any signal applied without bias will have to negotiate the S-bend halfway down and so become severely distorted. However, if the signal is superimposed on the high-frequency waveform as in Fig. 3.5 the centre kink will be avoided as both sides of the composite wave will be applied to the two straight portions of the characteristic. These are additive, so the result will be a signal at least twice as large as the d.c. system which uses only one portion of the characteristic, allowing a larger signal to be recorded. The a.c. system also produces less noise.

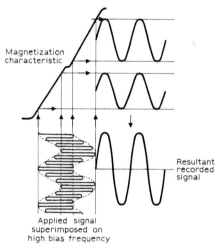

Fig. 3.5    If the superimposed waveform resulting from bias-plus-signal is applied to the combined magnetisation characteristic, the centre kink is avoided, resulting in the two undistorted waveforms which combine to give the resultant recorded signal.

## Bias Adjustment

The level of the bias waveform must be just right; if it is too low the superimposed signal will start to encroach on the curved centre part of the magnetisation characteristic and increase distortion; if it is too great, the higher signal frequencies will be attenuated. So the level is set to give freedom from distortion with the best possible high-frequency response. Different makes of tape have slightly different magnetisation characteristics, so, in theory, each one should have the bias level adjusted to suit. Professional recording machines have such a control with an indicator to measure the bias level.

Domestic recorders are not quite so critical and most makes of tape can be used with little noticeable difference. Even so, most recorders have an internal adjustment that can be set by an engineer. If one make of tape seems to give more distortion than others, the bias setting could be too low for it and be re-set to suit. However, this could affect recordings with other tapes, although the playback will not be affected.

Most domestic-type recorders are set as a compromise to give generally good results on most makes of tape, but it should be noted that manufacturers who also make tape set the bias to give best results on their *own* tape which sometimes differs from the characteristics of other tapes. This is why certain makes and types of tape are specified in instruction manuals.

### Frequency Response and Tape Speed

Tape speed has a bearing on frequency response. Imagine that the slit in the head-gap is a stencil and paint is being sprayed through it onto a moving surface on the other side. The paint is being turned on and off at a fixed number of times per minute. The result will be a series of bands of paint on the moving surface of equal width, providing the speed of the moving surface is constant.

Supposing now we speed up the frequency that the sprayer is turned on and off. The bands of colour will get narrower and closer together. Eventually, if we go on increasing the frequency the bands and the spacing between them will be as narrow as the slit, then any further increase in frequency will result in the start of the next band commencing before the trailing edge of the previous one is clear of the slit, and so they will overlap and form a continuous band.

In order to distinguish frequencies higher than this we can increase the speed of the moving surface so that the one band is past the slit before the next one starts, or we can reduce the width of the slit. The same thing applies to magnetic tape recording. There is an upper limit to the frequency that we can record at any given tape speed and head-gap width. Head-gaps have been getting progressively narrower as manufacturing techniques have improved over the years. Gaps of less than a hundredth of a millimetre are now quite common.

Given a certain gap width then, a fast tape speed will record higher frequencies than a slower one. The standard single-speed reel-to-reel machine runs at $3\frac{3}{4}$ inches per second, at which speed frequencies of up to 8kHz or 13kHz can be recorded, depending on head-gap and other design features. Most domestic machines will fall somewhere between these two upper limits. On modern 3-speed machines the extra speeds are $1\frac{7}{8}$i/S, at which frequencies of 4 to 7kHz are reached, and $7\frac{1}{2}$i/S at which frequencies up to 12 or 17kHz are obtainable.

## Excessive Frequency Response Claims

Some manufacturers claim a frequency response considerably in excess of these figures. This may be due to some genuine advance in design, such as *cross-field* bias in which the bias is applied to the tape from a separate head positioned at the back of the tape, giving a frequency response roughly equivalent to that obtainable at the next highest speed, with conventional biasing.

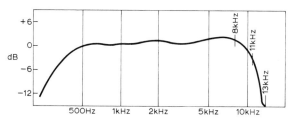

Fig. 3.6    Typical overall frequency response of a tape recorder operating at $3\frac{3}{4}$i/S. The upper limit could be defined as the point where the curve starts to drop (8kHz), where it falls to —6dB (11kHz), or the point where the response virtually ceases (13kHz).

However, one cannot achieve the impossible, so abnormal claims should be treated with suspicion. Fig. 3.6 shows a typical overall response of a recorder at $3\frac{3}{4}$i/S. Notice that at the upper end the drop-off is gradual. Hence one can quote the upper frequency limit as the point where the curve begins to fall off, or part way down, say where the response is 6dB below, or one can quote the frequency at the bottom of the curve, that is the highest frequency at which there is any response at all. This is so low as to be virtually non-existent, yet as there *is* a response there, a maker could quote it as the upper limit, in which case the performance would look a lot better than it really is.

## Equalising and High-frequency Boosting

The record head possesses the property of inductance, and this prevents it responding equally to electric currents of all frequencies. This, combined with magnetic and other losses which are greater at higher frequencies, means that the frequency response of the head itself is relatively constant only between about 1kHz and 5kHz. Above and below these figures there is a gradual decline, and to correct this the declining frequencies can be boosted in the amplifier. The high frequencies are boosted during recording, and the low frequencies boosted during playback, thus the overall response comes out level.

In order to reduce the effect of poor high-frequency response at the slower speeds, more treble boost is given, Unfortunately it also introduces a peak in the upper part of the characteristic, giving a false brilliance which can sometimes be rather harsh. This boosting of various frequencies to compensate for head losses and different speed characteristics is called *equalising,* and the frequencies and amount is subject to international agreement. This means that tapes recorded on one machine can be replayed on a machine of another make, or even from a different country of manufacture, providing the tracks are the same.

Manual tone controls are provided on most recorders. Where there is just a single control, this is usually a top-cut device which progressively reduces the high frequencies. Some recorders also have a bass-cut control which does the same for the low frequencies. On the more expensive models they are sometimes combined with boost controls; with these the centre position is 'flat', rotation giving cut in one direction and boost in the other. All tone controls operate only on playback to prevent them being accidentally moved during recording and thus spoiling it.

### How Many Tracks?

There is much misunderstanding among recorder users on the question of tracks. This has nothing to do with the tape itself but refers to a particular tape recorder, which may record either four narrow tracks or two wider ones. Once recorded, a tape must be played back on the same type of machine in order for it to correctly 'read' the tracks. However, if the tape is erased, it can be recorded again either as a 4-track or 2-track tape.

With the 2-track system, the head-gap is at the upper part of the head and it makes a track across the upper half of the tape. When the tape reaches its end the reels are changed over and this turns the tape upside down. The bottom half is now recorded by the same head gap, but in the opposite direction. (Fig. 3.7).

A 4-track head has two gaps, one at the top and the other underneath as shown in Fig. 3.8. A switch on the recorder can select either of these for recording or playback. When the tape is recorded to its end, the tape is turned upside-down as before by reversing the reels. Now the top gap records along the bottom edge, while the lower one is interleaved between the two previous ones. Thus tracks 1 and 3 are recorded in the forward direction and 2 and 4 in the reverse (Fig. 3.8).

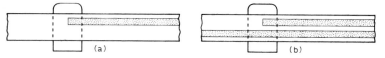

Fig. 3.7   (a) Top track being recorded on a 2-track recorder. (b) Tape reversed, enabling bottom track to be recorded.

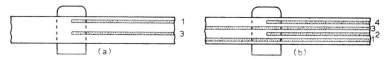

Fig. 3.8   (a) With four tracks, 1 and 3 are recorded in the forward direction. (b) tracks 2 and 4 are recorded in the reverse direction.

## Features of the Four-track System

The first and obvious advantage of the 4-track system is economy, as twice as much material can be recorded on a given length of tape, but because the track is narrower, the head output is less on playback than it would be on the 2-track system and the ratio between signal and amplifier noise is worse. Irregularities in the oxide deposit on the tape will have a greater effect on a narrow track than a wide one and this will also tend to increase noise levels.

If the edge of the tape parts company with the head during recording due to insufficient pressure or a kink or crease in the tape, even for an instant, there will be a momentary break in the recording. With a wide track, some part of the tape will still be in contact with the head, so the only effect will be a slight drop in level which will most likely pass unnoticed. In the case of a narrow track, the entire track may be interrupted, resulting in complete silence for the instant.

The 4-track system is obviously more prone to this effect (known as *drop-out*) which mostly affects the tracks nearest the edge of the tape, i.e. tracks 1 and 4. When using a 4-track machine to record an important item where good quality is essential, the inner tracks (either 2 or 3) should always be used because of the reduced possibility of drop-out.

For creative tape recording, editing the tape is often carried out, and will ruin any other track which may be recorded, so tapes likely to be edited should be recorded on only one track. Therefore, the principal advantage of the 4-track system is nullified for the creative recordist, while the disadvantages remain. However, with 4-track

machines, duo-play and sound-on-sound provide the possibility of
multiple recordings, useful for the creative recordist, and these are
discussed in Chapter 11.

**Playback**

With most recorders, the recording head is also used for playback.
When the track with its magnetic variations is made to pass over the
head gap, a varying field is induced in the head-core which in turn
produces a corresponding electric current in the winding. It is very
weak and needs considerable amplification before it can be applied to
the loudspeaker.

The head signal is usually fed to the preamplifier stage of the
amplifier used for recording, the input sockets and recording level
indicator being switched out and the tone control switched in. Also. the
oscillator which generates the recording bias is switched off. In some
earlier recorders the valve which functioned as the oscillator is
switched to drive the loudspeaker during playback. Where a separate
valve is used, it often provides the facility of monitoring the recording
through the loudspeaker. The equalising circuits are also switched
from boosting the treble during recording to boosting the bass while in
playback. All this happens when you depress the Playback button!

The more expensive recorders employ separate heads and amplifiers
for recording and playback so that each can be designed and constructed for optimum performance instead of being a compromise
between the varying requirement of the two functions. Also the complicated switching is eliminated. The use of separate heads permits
direct monitoring from the tape during recording, and machines
incorporating this feature usually include an A-B monitor switch,
whereby the signals entering the recorder can be monitored in the A
position, and the actual recording from the playback head can be heard
in the B position. Switching from one to the other provides a revealing
test of recorded quality.

**Erasing**

Erasure is an important function of tape recording, permitting an
unwanted recording to be 'rubbed out' and the tape used again. This
can be done time and time again with no deterioration of the tape or
quality of the subsequent recordings. In the saturation method, the tape
is heavily magnetised by means of a permanent magnet or a d.c. current
flowing through an erase head, obliterating any existing magnetic
patterns.

In zero erasure, a large high-frequency a.c. current is passed through the erase head, producing a corresponding magnetic field which demagnetises the tape and thus removes any existing magnetic recording. The current is obtained from the oscillator that supplies bias for the recording head, but it is much greater. The saturation method, although cheaper and easier to arrange, is inferior to the zero erasing system as the magnetised tape tends to be more noisy.

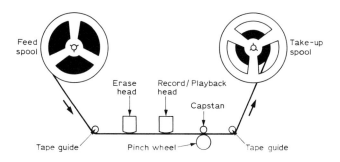

Fig. 3.9   Basic tape transport path showing sequence of components.

## The Erase Head

In either case, the erase head must be carefully aligned in relation to the record head. The gap must be lined up so that it follows the track made by the record head exactly, otherwise part of the recorded track would remain un-erased, and in a bad case of misalignment part of another track may be erased. Adjustment of the height and vertical inclination of each head is possible by means of set screws around its base, but these must only be adjusted in accordance with a proper alignment procedure, and using a test tape.

The erase head is on the left-hand side looking at the recorder from the front, so that the tape passes over it before reaching the record head. When making a new recording on a tape which is already recorded it is not necessary to erase the tape first because when the instrument is switched to Record, the erase head is in circuit and any previous recording is automatically wiped off the tape.

To reduce the possibility of tapes being erased by switching to Record instead of Playback, most recorders incorporate some mechanical interlocking arrangement so that it is impossible to press the Record key without pressing a Release key at the same time. With some instruments, pressing the Start control operates the machine in the playback mode; to record, both Record button and Start key must be depressed simultaneously.

Some recorders have a switch to render the erase head inoperative during recording to allow the new recording to be superimposed on the old one to make a composite recording. Of course, if the new recording is unsatisfactory the old one is spoiled as there is no way of erasing one without the other. Furthermore, the applied recording bias for the new recording tends to remove the high frequencies from the old one, so it sounds somewhat muffled in comparison with the new.

### External Speakers

During playback, the tape can be heard over the internal loudspeaker. Because most recorders are 'portable', the size of the speaker and its baffle is limited, and this curtails the low frequencies and can introduce rattles and resonances if the volume is turned up. Recordings are not usually heard to full advantage through the internal loudspeaker, especially if music is involved, and most models provide a socket for plugging in an external loudspeaker. Inserting the plug in the speaker socket usually mutes the internal speaker.

Playback can also be improved by the use of an external hi-fi amplifier and speaker. To facilitate this, a socket is provided on some recorders marked *Amplifier* or *Line*. This is tapped from an early stage of the internal amplifier, and so the signal does not pass through the stages driving the loudspeaker, which are the ones that contribute the most distortion.

### Mechanical Aspects

The first and obvious mechanical requirement is to move the tape at a steady speed from left to right across the erase and record/playback heads. Any speed variation, either during recording or playback, will cause a corresponding change of pitch in the sound. Drive is effected by means of a steel spindle of uniform diameter against which the tape is pressed by a rubber jockey-wheel. This spindle has a flywheel fitted to its lower portion which ensures that it revolves at a more or less constant speed free from short-term fluctuations. However, any unbalance in the flywheel or fault in the bearings may cause a regular speed variation known as *wow*. The efficiency of the flywheel in smoothing out speed variations depends on its mass and speed. Variations are therefore greater on machines that have small, light, flywheels such as most portable battery recorders.

The flywheel is driven from the motor by a small rubber idler wheel which bears against both flywheel rim and motor spindle, or by a belt which encircles the flywheel and motor spindle. The idler wheel can become hard with age and introduce knocking sounds, as well as producing speed variations. Belts are silent, but are prone to stretch, resulting in slow-running and speed variation.

On 3-speed machines, the motor spindle is fitted with a stepped capstan having three diameters. The idler wheel is made to engage with the appropriate one by means of the speed control lever. Belt drives are less usual with 3-speed models because of the difficulty of making the belt jump from one diameter pulley to another, and the differences of tension that would exist at different diameters. However, several 2-speed models employ belts.

The faster the speed, the more effective is the flywheel, therefore wow and other speed variations are less troublesome at the higher speeds. Thus recording at the faster speeds confers the advantage of a

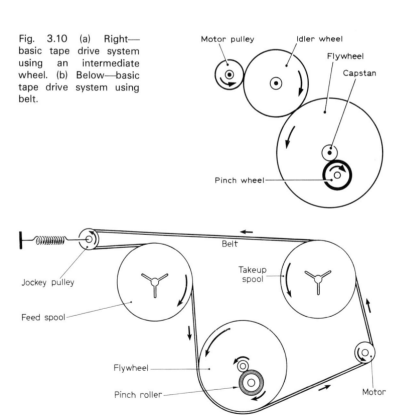

Fig. 3.10 (a) Right— basic tape drive system using an intermediate wheel. (b) Below—basic tape drive system using belt.

better high-frequency response, as we have seen, plus a more stable speed.

## Pressure Pads

It is necessary for the tape to be in intimate contact with both erase and recording heads and this can be achieved by means of a pressure pad, usually of felt, which gently presses the tape against the heads. These pads (one for each head) are sometimes mounted on a swinging arm which also supports the rubber jockey or pinch wheel. On pressing the Start key, this arm swings toward the heads, causing the tape to be presented to the heads and also to be pressed against the drive spindle by the pinch wheel. Alternatively, the pads (on flaps or plates) are pivoted into contact with the tape by the action of the Start selector.

If the pressure exerted by the pads is too weak, the tape may lift away giving rise to drop-out, but if too heavy, excessive drag will be introduced, slowing the speed and causing premature wear to the face of the heads. Pressure is usually maintained at the right level by means of a light spring on the pad supports.

If the pads become hard and caked with dirt and oxide from the tape, they tend to bind or hold the tape momentarily, so that the tape proceeds past the heads in a succession of very rapid jerks. The effect, known as *flutter,* is not always readily detectable as a form of speed variation, but the reproduction sounds distorted and rather 'bubbly' as though it were being played under water. This may also be accompanied by a squeak from the pad.

An alternative tape-to-head contact is effected by shaping, i.e. contouring the heads so that the tape, in its travel, wraps partly around the heads, obviating the need for pressure pads.

## Tape Take-up

In addition to pulling the tape past the heads at a constant speed, the recorder must take it onto the right-hand spool. This is not just a case of directly driving the spool from the motor. The spool revolves quickly when it is empty at the start of the tape, but fills up as the playing continues, each revolution accommodating a greater length of tape. As the tape itself is running at constant speed, the take-up spool must revolve ever slower until, when it is full, it is turning at a fraction of the speed that it was at the start.

To drive it at this gradually decreasing speed, a slipping friction drive is used. The spool carrier is made up of two sections, the lower part being driven by belt or idler wheel from the motor, and the upper part driven from the lower one by light friction, usually by means of a felt washer or ring between them. Light pressure between them to provide the drive is maintained by gravity (the weight of the upper part and the tape spool) or by a spring. The use of a spring means that the drive is independent of gravity, and so the recorder can be operated in a position other than horizontal.

At the start of the tape when the spool is revolving at maximum speed, the upper and lower parts turn together, but as the speed decreases, the top part slips relative to the lower. Thus the top part and the spool will turn only as fast as the tape coming from the drive spindle will allow. There is therefore always tension on the tape, between the spindle and the take-up spool, which gives a firm and neat lay to the tape. Tape coming from the other spool is simply pulled off by the drive spindle, tension being that caused by the inertia of the spool. Some types of drive also employ a clutched feed spool, giving a light back tension to avoid tape spillage and the possibility of 'flutter'.

Some of the more expensive recorders employ three motors, one to drive the tape and the others to drive the two spool-carriers. In this case, the take-up spool motor is operated at reduced power or torque by limiting the current to it. The drive is direct from the motor, but it will only turn as fast as the tape will allow as in the case of the friction drive in the single-motor recorders. No damage to the tape results from this because of the low torque generated by the motor.

## Fast Rewind

The third essential mechanical function of a tape recorder is to rewind the tape onto the original spool at high speed, and also to wind forward so that parts of the recording near the end can be quickly located. Some battery recorders omit the latter facility and only provide rewind.

Both functions are quite straightforward. With 3-motor decks, the appropriate motor is switched on and the other two off. Alternatively, the motor for the turntable from which the tape is being fed may be run at reduced torque to maintain even winding. The series resistor for reducing the torque of the take-up spool is shorted out on fast-forward to provide the maximum power. In single-motor recorders, the motor is made to drive either spool via idler wheel or belts with low-ratio gearing so that a fast speed is obtained. In the case of the take-up spool, the upper and lower portions of the carrier are locked together in order that there will be no slipping and loss of drive.

A further mechanical facility, not provided on all machines, is the revolution counter. This is usually a small unit similar to a mileometer, which is belt-driven from one of the spool carriers. It gives an approximate reference so that required portions of the tape can be found again easily. It must be set to zero at the start of each recording by means of a knurled thumb-wheel or press-to-reset button. During fast-forwarding or rewinding, slippage takes place in the belt drive so the setting is never the same as it is when the tape is running normally. Settings must always therefore be considered as approximate. Some counters provide a 3-digit readout, but a 4-digit counter is an advantage if lengthy tapes are likely to be used.

This has necessarily been a rather cursory review of the principles of tape recording. Enthusiasts requiring a more detailed treatment are refered to *Tape Recorders,* by H. W. Hellyer, published by Fountain Press.

# CHAPTER FOUR

# CHOOSING THE EQUIPMENT

THE TYPE OF EQUIPMENT REQUIRED by the creative tape recordist will depend on what fields of activity are to be pursued. If a tape recorder is already available but the facilities are too limited it could be part-exchanged for a more suitable instrument or kept as a second recorder, which is often very useful. Creative recordings can be made on a modest instrument, but more ingenuity may have to be used to obtain satisfactory results.

**Choose a Mains Recorder**

The principal tape recorder should be mains operated. The heavier motor and larger flywheel give a much better speed constancy than all but the top-flight battery units. Additionally, all mains models employ a.c. recording bias and erasure. Many battery models do, too, but it is not always possible to be certain even from the maker's handbook. The use of a.c. recording bias permits a higher signal level to be recorded, and as with the a.c. erasure, gives a more silent background.

A further advantage of mains recorders is that most of them can accommodate spool sizes up to 7″ diameter whereas most battery and battery/mains models can take only 5″ spools, some only $3\frac{1}{2}$″ spools. Combined mains/battery recorders must be considered to be battery machines that will also run off the mains, rather than mains instruments. This is because the need to conserve current when using batteries necessitates the use of small motors and reel sizes.

**Cassette Recorders**

Cassette recorders are now both common and popular. Several types of cassette have been produced, but the Philips Compact Cassette type seems to have ousted the others, and is the one in general use.

A cassette consists of two small reel hubs with the tape permanently threaded between them, mounted in a flat oblong case. Included also is a pair of springs on which are mounted the pressure pads for erase and record heads. The cassette is merely snapped into place on the machine, and pressing the Start control moves the heads forward to engage with the tape which is exposed along a slot at one edge of the cassette.

Playing times are 60, 90 or 120 minutes depending on tape thickness. Tape width is $\frac{1}{8}''$, half the width of normal tape. Advantages are ease of operation and tape changing, but disadvantages include lower signal/noise ratio due to smaller track width. Creative recording involves cutting and editing, not so easy as with open reels. The low tape speed of $1\frac{7}{8}$ i/S restricts the frequency response. Furthermore, various trick effects and fast copying are not possible with the single-speed cassette recorder. Although excellent for many applications, it is not recommended for serious creative recording.

Note that although it has been stated that tape width is $\frac{1}{8}''$, this is a nominal figure and the actual tape width is 0·015″.

### Reel Size and Tape Length

Many recorder owners find reel sizes, tape thicknesses and playing times rather confusing. The best way of sorting the matter out is to relate playing time to *tape length* rather than reel size. Remember that 1,200 feet of tape will run for an hour at the standard speed of $3\frac{3}{4}$ i/S. (Actually the time is nearer 65 minutes). All other sizes can then be easily worked out for standard reel lengths. There are also 150-foot

Fig. 4.1   A modern versatile tape deck featuring mixing, monitoring, multi-play and echo facilities (Philips model N4500).

Fig. 4.2 (left) The National R0209DSE, typical of the less expensive cassette tape recorders.

Fig. 4.3 (right) The Uher Stereo 124, one of a growing range of more sophisticated cassette recorders.

reels ('message' reels) that will run for about 7 minutes, and at the other end of the scale, 2,400- and 3,600-foot spools that will give 2 hours and 3 hours respectively. These times are for *each track*, so total playing-time capacity of a tape will depend on whether the recorder is a 2- or 4-track instrument. However, for an uninterrupted run, the track time is the one that matters.

*Standard-thickness* tape needs a 7-inch reel to hold 1,200 feet, a $5\frac{3}{4}$-inch spool will hold 900 feet, while 600 feet can be accommodated on a 5-inch reel. A 4-inch reel (not very common) will hold 300 feet while the 3-inch will house 150 feet.

*Long-play* tape gives approximately half as much again length of tape for a given reel size. Thus 1,800 feet will go on a 7-inch reel, 1,200 feet on a $5\frac{3}{4}$-inch reel, 900 feet on a 5-inch, 450 on a 4-inch, and 210 feet on a 3-inch spool. With *double-play* tape twice as much tape can be accommodated on a reel as with standard tape. 2,400 feet on a 7-inch reel and so on.

The thinnest tape in common use is *triple play*, of which three times the length of standard tape will be housed on the same sized reels. There are some odd reel sizes used with triple-play tape to give extended playing times on smaller machines, such as the $3\frac{1}{4}$-inch reel which will hold 600 feet, giving a full half-an-hour per track at $3\frac{3}{4}$ i/S. Most battery recorders taking a 3-inch maximum reel will accommodate the extra $\frac{1}{4}$-inch reel size. Also there is a $4\frac{1}{4}$-inch reel which holds 1,200 feet of triple-play, this being intended for normal 4-inch maximum machines. There is also a *quadruple-play* tape but it is little needed, except to get very long playing times from battery recorders. It is not usually stocked by tape retailers, and it is expensive.

When calculating playing times, reel sizes and tape thicknesses can confuse matters. All tapes have the *length* printed on the box in addition to the reel size and tape thickness. It matters not that 1,200 feet of tape is wound as standard tape on a 7-inch reel, or as long-play tape on a $5\frac{3}{4}$-inch reel, or as double-play on a 5-inch reel, or even as triple play on a $4\frac{1}{4}$-inch reel; it will still run for an hour at $3\frac{3}{4}$ i/S.

Reel sizes and tape thicknesses do have to be considered, however, when the capacity of a machine is a limiting factor. For example, to obtain an hour's recording with a maximum recorder reel size of $5\frac{3}{4}$ inches, long-play or thinner tape is necessary. Models taking 7-inch spools present no problem as any size will go on. Remember, too, that you may wish to play recordings made by someone else, and these may come on a 7-inch spool.

## Features of Thinner Tapes

Thinner tapes are more flexible and so take the contours of the recording head more readily. This, particularly with 4-track machines, is an advantage inasmuch as it reduces the incidence of drop-out. In fact it has been found that machines that are prone to drop-out become relatively free from it when a thinner tape is used.

Longer playing time is not so important with machines taking large spools, but it is a consideration with battery recorders with which only very short recordings can be made with thicker tapes. To reduce the mechanical load on the motor, which is low-powered to conserve battery current, pressures and tensions are much less in battery instruments than their mains counterparts. Hence, in order to achieve intimate tape-to-head contact the thinner, more flexible, tapes should be used.

The thinner tapes, however, are more likely to break or stretch. This does not normally occur during recording or playback, but some machines impose quite high stresses when rewinding or fast-forwarding, especially those which have three motors and, as a result, a very fast rewind. The most dangerous time for tape breakage is when stopping part-way through a rewind or fast-forward. Both spool carriers have brakes, but if these operate unevenly so that the paying-out spool stops more suddenly than the take-up spool, then strain and possible breakage will result. This can happen even when the brakes are equally effective if there is much more tape on one spool than on the other, or one reel is bigger than the other.

The thinner tapes, then, can be prone to breakage on machines with fast rewind characteristics, but are relatively safe on slower machines. Battery recorders are quite slow in rewind so there will be little danger of damage from this source. As a rough guide to the rewind time category, taking 1,800 feet of tape as the standard length in each case, 5 minutes or more is slow (common with most popular single-motor

| Tape Thickness | Spool Dia. (in.) | Tape Length (ft) | Playing Time per track (minutes at speed per sec.) | | |
|---|---|---|---|---|---|
| | | | $1\frac{7}{8}''$ | $3\frac{3}{4}''$ | $7\frac{1}{2}''$ |
| **Standard Tape** | 5 | 600 | 60 | 30 | 15 |
| | $5\frac{3}{4}$ | 900 | 90 | 45 | $22\frac{1}{2}$ |
| | 7 | 1200 | 120 | 60 | 30 |
| | $8\frac{1}{4}$ | 1800 | 180 | 90 | 45 |
| **Long Play Tape** | 3 | 210 | 22 | 11 | $5\frac{1}{2}$ |
| | 4 | 450 | 45 | $22\frac{1}{2}$ | 11 |
| | $4\frac{1}{4}$ | 600 | 60 | 30 | 15 |
| | 5 | 900 | 90 | 45 | $22\frac{1}{2}$ |
| | $5\frac{3}{4}$ | 1200 | 120 | 60 | 30 |
| | 7 | 1800 | 180 | 90 | 45 |
| | $8\frac{1}{4}$ | 2400 | 240 | 120 | 60 |
| | 10 | 3600 | 360 | 180 | 90 |
| **Double Play Tape** | 3 | 300 | 30 | 15 | $7\frac{1}{2}$ |
| | 4 | 600 | 60 | 30 | 15 |
| | $4\frac{1}{4}$ | 900 | 90 | 45 | $22\frac{1}{2}$ |
| | 5 | 1200 | 120 | 60 | 30 |
| | $5\frac{3}{4}$ | 1800 | 180 | 90 | 45 |
| | 7 | 2400 | 240 | 120 | 60 |
| **Triple Play Tape** | 3 | 450 | 45 | $22\frac{1}{2}$ | 11 |
| | 4 | 900 | 90 | 45 | $22\frac{1}{2}$ |
| | $4\frac{1}{4}$ | 1200 | 120 | 60 | 30 |
| | 5 | 1800 | 180 | 90 | 45 |
| | $5\frac{3}{4}$ | 2400 | 240 | 120 | 60 |
| | 7 | 3600 | 360 | 180 | 90 |

Table 4.1  Tape Playing Times

| Tape Speeds | | Tape Spool Sizes | |
|---|---|---|---|
| 15in./S | 38·1cm* | 7 inches | 17·5cm |
| $7\frac{1}{2}$in./S | 19·1cm* | $5\frac{3}{4}$ inches | 14·6cm |
| $3\frac{3}{4}$in./S | 9·5cm. | 5 inches | 12·7cm |
| $1\frac{7}{8}$in./S | 4·8cm* | 4 inches | 10·2cm |
| $\frac{15}{16}$in./ S | 2·4cm | 3 inches | 7·6cm |

\* accepted figures are 38, 19 and 4·75cms respectively.

1 inch=2·54cm   1 mil=25μ (microns).   1μ (micron)=0·00004in.
1 thou'=0·001in.=25·4μ   1cm=0·3937 inches (0·4in. approx.)

Table 4.2  Metric Conversions

decks), 3 minutes is sometimes achieved with single-motor decks and is a good speed, $1\frac{1}{2}$ minutes is fast and only attained by 3-motor decks.

## Print-through

When tapes are stored for any length of time an effect known as *print through* sometimes occurs. The magnetic pattern on one layer of tape affects the adjacent layer and magnetises it to the same pattern. The result is an echo following the original sound if the affected layer is beneath the magnetising one on the spool, or a pre-echo with the spurious sound coming before the original if the layer is above.

In either case, the spurious signal is weak and may not be detected, but in some circumstances such as a sudden loud sound followed or preceded by silence, echo or pre-echo may be heard. One method of avoiding this is to periodically rewind your tapes whether they are played or not, so that adjacent layers will not be in exactly the same relative position as before. This also helps to prevent the tape curling, which otherwise can happen during storage.

Print-through is more likely to occur when the adjacent layers of magnetic material are close together. As they are separated only by the thickness of the tape itself, it follows that the risk of print-through is greater with the thinner tapes and if it does occur it will be worse.

The thin tapes are more expensive than the standard ones of the same length, so triple-play tapes are the most expensive, double-play the next and so on.

## Which Tape?

Which is the best tape to use? For a 2-track machine with large spool capacity, long-play tapes will generally prove the most satisfactory. They have just that little more flexibility than standard tapes, yet retain adequate strength and are not greatly susceptible to print-through. Up to $1\frac{1}{2}$ hours per track can be recorded at $3\frac{3}{4}$ i/S (1,800 feet, the maximum for a 7-inch spool) which will usually be sufficient for a single uninterrupted recording. Yet the cost is not very much more than an equivalent length of standard tape.

For most 4-track machines, long-play tape will also prove the best proposition, but if drop-out is being experienced, and the pressure pad is in order, it may be necessary to use double-play. Normally double- and triple-play tape will be used on battery machines where a really flexible tape and a long playing-time from small reels is required.

Fig. 4.4 A selection of mains-operated tape recorders: (top left) the Tandberg Series 15SL, (top right) the Uher 714, (bottom right) the Van Der Molen VR7T.

## Two or Four Tracks?

Creative recording involves cutting and editing tape, and this renders useless any other recordings on other tracks. So, while 4-track machines are economical for making continuous un-edited recordings, this is not the case with creative work. Also the noise level is higher, they are slightly more expensive and are more prone to drop-out.

Multiplay facilities (the adding of other sounds to a recording) can only be obtained on 4-track machines, something in their favour, as this has numerous creative possibilities. However, relatively few 4-track machines include this, and it is possible to rig up a multiplay set-up using two separate 2-track recorders.

## Monitoring

The ability to monitor the signal while recording is very useful. Some expensive machines have a separate head and playback amplifier so that the actual tape recording can be heard while it is being recorded. The loudspeaker can be switched from this to the signal coming into the recorder, so that the two can be instantaneously compared. However, tape monitoring is something of a refinement, but monitoring the incoming signal is almost a 'must', and is included even in many inexpensive instruments.

Monitoring may be by means of the internal loudspeaker, the volume control used for playback also controlling the monitor. The sound quality is not quite the same as during playback because the signal passes through the amplifier which is switched to the Record position in which equalising circuits are used to compensate for the tape frequency characteristics. Hence, bass will be deficient and treble over-emphasised, but the general quality can be assessed if it is remembered that the playing of the actual recording will sound more balanced.

Some instruments include a monitoring facility for which headphones are needed. This may not always be quite so convenient, but in some cases loudspeaker monitoring is undesirable and headphones preferred. Machines providing loudspeaker monitoring usually include facilities for headphone monitoring as well.

## Pause Control

This enables a temporary halt to be made to either recording or playback without using the 'Stop' control. If the Stop control is used during recording the interlocking latch on the Record button or key returns to zero and the machine reverts to the playback condition. To restart, these must be reset to Record. This can be a nuisance if the pause is a short one but, what is worse, switching to Record often produces a click on the recording.

The pause function is purely mechanical; the pinch wheel is held off from the drive spindle and brakes are applied to the spool carriers. When the control is released, recording continues without a break or any switching noise. The ability to do this is extremely useful in creative recording, so it should be regarded as a necessary facility.

A point to watch, however, is that some pause controls have to be held in position during the pause. This is a disadvantage because adjustments or work on associated equipment is often necessary during the pause, and this is difficult with one hand engaged. There is a danger, too, of pressure on the control being partially released thereby allowing an inch or two of tape to go past the heads and unwanted material being recorded. The best type of pause controls are those that lock in position, leaving both hands free.

## How Many Speeds

Most recordings will be made at the standard speed of $3\frac{3}{4}$ i/S (that of single-speed models), even if a 3-speed machine is used. The faster speed of $7\frac{1}{2}$ i/S is intended for high quality work, usually live music, while the slower speed of $1\frac{7}{8}$ i/S is for maximum economy when recording long periods of speech such as dictation, meeting proceedings, etc. The latter would hardly come under the creative category, and the former would not often be used.

Even so, 3-speed machines have advantages. It may be necessary for example to copy a tape that has been heavily edited and contains many splices, in order to preserve it in more durable form on an uncut tape, or to use as an entry for a tape-club competition, etc. Now if the original recording is made at $3\frac{3}{4}$ i/S, but re-recorded at $7\frac{1}{2}$ i/S, the copy will be made in half the time. Copies of $1\frac{7}{8}$ i/S recordings can be made at $7\frac{1}{2}$ i/S in a quarter of the time.

On location, recordings may be made with a battery portable running at $1\frac{7}{8}$ i/S, and better quality reproduction enjoyed by playing it back on the main 3-speed machine. Special effects can be made by recording sound sources at one speed and playing back at another, and this will be discussed in Chapter 7. We must consider, too, that the recorder may be required from time to time for more mundane purposes, business and domestic, and a selection of speeds may be very useful. So, a 3-speed machine, although not essential for creative recording, can be a great asset.

### Control Layout

General layout and type of controls should be taken into consideration when purchasing a recorder. Some have been carefully designed with regard to the ease and convenience of operation, while others have not. Press keys with a centrally positioned Stop key larger than the others and the Record key a distinctive colour are probably the ideal arrangement. If the Rewind key is on the extreme left and the Fast-forward key on the extreme right, these operations will be easier to perform, because the fingers will go naturally to these positions.

With the Volume, Record-level and Tone controls, it is useful if there is some means of indicating their setting with divisions or inscribed numbers around them. It is then possible to alter a setting and return to the original one later. Or when mixing two sound sources, test recordings can be made at different levels and the settings noted.

Some recorders have only a mark on the knob to indicate position while others have plain knobs with no indication at all. A machine should not be rejected on this score if it is satisfactory in other respects. Knobs can easily be removed and replaced by a more useful type with arrow type pointers moulded in or a flange on which numbers are inscribed.

**Desirable Features**

A facility important for creative recording is the provision of both Microphone and Gram input socket, each with their separate controls. It will often be necessary to mix two sound sources—a microphone with the output of a gramophone record or, more usually, another tape recorder. Most recorders have both sockets but if there is only a microphone socket, a separate mixer will be required.

A minor but rather annoying habit of some manufacturers is to provide only a tiny space for stowing the microphone and mains cable. Quite often the fitting of a 13 amp 3-pin plug (the standard flat-pin plug now in common use) makes it impossible to pack the lead into its compartment.

The instrument chosen should have a good frequency response but beware of misleading figures. A good-sized loudspeaker in a solid wooden cabinet or case will give better reproduction than a tiny one in a plastics case. However, on playback, an external loudspeaker mounted in a large cabinet can be plugged into the recorder, or better still, a hi-fi amplifier may be connected to the socket provided for this purpose on some tape recorders. This mutes the internal speaker and its output stage and gives the maximum quality.

If it is not intended to use either an external amplifier or loudspeaker, then make sure that the internal one is good enough for serious listening. When the recorder is being demonstrated, listen for a good bass response and freedom from rattles and buzzes at high volume levels as these are the most common deficiencies.

**A Second Recorder**

There are many occasions when a second tape recorder is needed, as when extracting and assembling parts of other tapes without cutting the originals, adding sound effects from other recordings, making multiple 2-track recordings or simply making straight copies. One can, of course, borrow a second recorder from a friend, but a lengthy project may require the use of two instruments for a considerable time. Extravagant though it may seem, the answer is to own a second machine. This need not be a top quality model and could be second-hand, but it will certainly prove worthwhile in the making of creative recordings.

It should be able to accept 7-inch reels, otherwise its usefulness will be limited. If its use is confined to playing tapes for recording on the first machine, it need have no monitoring facilities and as in most cases the copying will be by direct-wire connection between the two recorders it need not have a good loudspeaker or substantial baffle area. A

Fig. 4.5 A selection of portable reel-to-reel tape recorders: (top left) Grundig TK3200 mains/battery model with automatic/manual level control, (top right) the Sony model TC222, (below) the 3-head Nagra IV-L favoured by professionals.

pause control is useful, and it would be an advantage to have a 3-speed machine to permit high-speed copying. The second machine should have the same number of tracks as the first if recordings are to be compatible.

**Battery Recorders**

Even with two machines, recording is dependent on access to a mains supply. Battery recorders are unsuitable as the main instrument, but they can prove valuable to supplement the others, as many recording opportunities occur outdoors. So three instruments are really desirable if full use is to be made of the many opportunities for creative recording.

Fortunately, battery recorders are relatively inexpensive, but there are a number of desirable features. Both a.c. bias and erasure should be employed. Spools are preferrable to cassettes, popular though the latter may be, because they can then be played on the mains machines, and can be more easily edited.

Many foreign battery recorders employ a simple speed-change device. The basic speed is $1\frac{7}{8}$ i/S, but if $3\frac{3}{4}$ i/S is required, a sleeve is slipped over the tape-drive spindle and held in place by a thumbscrew. This increases the diameter of the spindle and so increases the speed. There is no adjustment of electronic equalising by this method, but the improved frequency response and reduction in wow and flutter of the faster speed is useful, whereas the slower speed is handy when long playing times are required.

Another convenient feature of many imported machines is that an on/off switch is incorporated in the microphone. This enables the recorder to be set up and switched to Record, then switched off by the microphone switch. To start recording immediately one simply flicks the switch.

**Automatic Control**

Some tape recorders include an automatic recording level control facility. In normal operation the recording level must be carefully set by watching the modulation indicator. When recording outdoors close attention cannot always be given to this and sound levels can vary suddenly without warning. The automatic control circuit takes care of this by keeping the signal applied to the recording head below the maximum.

The dynamic range is compressed in the process as the relationship between loud and soft sounds is altered. Hence the auto-control should be used only when really needed, which is why many recorders incorporating it also include provision to switch over to manual control when required. The facility adds to the cost, of course, but is worth it, although it is not indispensable. As so many recording opportunities are to be found outdoors, it may well be wise to invest in a battery recorder instead of the second mains one if funds will not allow for all three.

**Second-Hand Machines**

Within limits, tape recorders do not deteriorate much with age, so it is possible to get one in first-class condition for a bargain price. Dealers sometimes have them, and the small ads in the newspapers and specialist magazines are other sources. When buying second-hand recorders, first check the condition of the heads. The constant passage of the tape produces wear on the face and the effect is to enlarge or distort the gap, which in turn causes a reduction of the high-frequency response.

This wear is usually discernible by a visual examination. In most models, the heads are protected by a cover which can be easily removed, usually by pulling upward. After removing the cover, examine the heads, especially the record/playback head, in a good light, and if possible view them with the light coming from a side-angle so that the contours stand out. The face of the head should have a smooth bevel over its entire area. A worn head will have a 'flat' worn at the front where the tape passes over the gap. In bad cases it may have a groove the width of the tape cut across the face (Fig. 4.6).

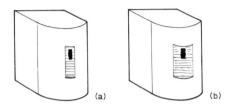

Fig. 4.6    (a) Tape record head exhibiting some wear. (b) a case of serious wear in which it appears that a "flat" has been filed across the face of the head. In both cases the ridge at the top and bottom of the worn area is more pronounced than at the side (which may be quite smooth).

A slight amount of wear only should be expected with well-cared-for machines, but if the heads are badly worn, this does not necessarily mean that the instrument is a bad buy. New heads are obtainable from the makers for a few pounds each and are easily fitted and adjusted by a skilled engineer, so fitting charges should not be high. Of course, it must be borne in mind that badly worn heads mean the instrument has had a lot of use, hence other parts also may need replacement.

While the head cover is off, look at the rest of the tape path. Heads may be replaced, but guides seldom. The amount of wear on these will therefore give a good indication of the use the machine has received. There may be fluff and brown tape dust around the bottom of the heads and guides. These accumulations are quite normal and can easily be brushed out with a special brush. However, if the recorder is being sold by a dealer who claims to have overhauled it, take note that any engineer worth his salt cleans out the head area when doing an overhaul.

If access can be obtained to the rubber pinch wheel, press it gently with the finger-nail. It should be firm yet resilient, 'giving' very slightly with the pressure of the nail but restoring immediately the pressure is released. If it is hard and will not give, or is spongy, then not only does it need replacing, a minor job in itself, but it casts doubt on the other rubber components, idler wheels and the like.

## Running Tests

After a visual examination of the case, lid, etc., check the mechanical operation and tape handling. The tape should be fed into the middle of the reel as shown in Fig. 4.7 not as shown at (a) where either the heads and guides are incorrectly positioned as to height above the deck, or the spool carrier has dropped. In this condition, the tape will rub on the spool cheek and may cause wow. Check that the position is right for normal playing or recording, and does not foul the cheeks on rewind and fast-forward, although on some machines the position may be slightly different as the spool carriers are lowered during fast forward or backward running.

   Rewind a full spool of tape right to the end to see that the rewind is working properly. It is at the end, when the take-up spool is full and the paying-out spool nearly empty, that the maximum load is imposed on the drive system and things sometimes begin to slow down. This is normal with some models, but if the slowing is very apparent and the reels come almost to a stop, there is a fault in the clutch, drive belt or motor (a rather expensive trouble to rectify). Try stopping and restarting several times during rewind to see that the tape is not damaged by faulty brakes, and also that the system can provide enough power to restart, especially near the end of the tape. This test should be repeated with the recorder set to Fast-forward.

## Checking the Speed

It is desirable to check the speed of the tape during normal running, $3\frac{3}{4}$i/S for a single-speed mains machine and half and double that for the three-speed models. If the speed is wrong there will be little effect on recordings made and played back on the same machine, of course, but when playing tapes made on another machine, or recording tapes made to be played back on another machine, speed and pitch differences will be noticed.

   Some recorders tend to run slow after a period of use, and while the trouble may be easily rectified by a competent engineer, the fault may be due to a number of components, including the motor, and prove difficult and expensive to correct. The most convenient way of checking the speed is by means of a stroboscope, a wheel with a channel in the rim for the tape to run in and alternate black and white segments

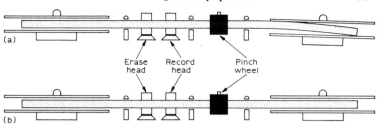

Fig. 4.7 (a) Side view of tape path with the take-up spool cheek fouling the tape due to the spool carrier being too low. (b) Correct alignment of spools and other components.

marked on the face. The wheel is supported on a bracket which also serves as a handle. There are other types of construction, but the principle is the same (Fig. 4.8).

A loop of tape is pulled from the machine between the drive spindle and the take-up spool and passed around the wheel (some makers advise pulling the loop from between the paying-out spool and the drive spindle, but tension is not always sufficient for the tape to give a firm drive to the strobe wheel). The tape is then set in motion and the wheel revolves. If it is running at the correct speed, the segments will appear to stand still when viewed in electric light (a.c. supply mains), fluorescent lighting being the best. If a large proportion of daylight is falling on the wheel as well, the effect is diminished and it may be difficult to distinguish the stationary pattern.

If the pattern appears to be moving in the same direction as the wheel (anti-clockwise), the tape is running fast, but if it seems to be going in the other direction, the tape is slow. Only with the more expensive models would one expect the speed to be spot-on, and a slight drift in either direction can be considered normal. Many new

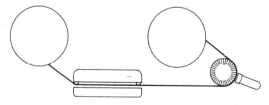

Fig. 4.8 Stroboscope in use. A loop of tape is pulled from between the heads and the take-up spool. The speed is correct when the pattern appears to be stationary when viewed in 50 Hz electric light.

machines, in fact, are found to run slightly fast, probably to allow for slowing up with age. On the other hand some new machines run a little slow due to the friction of bearings that have not 'run in' yet, and after some hours' use, the speed comes up to normal.

### Recording and Playback Tests

Now we must find out what the recorder sounds like. Switch to Playback and turn the volume to maximum with no tape running. Hum and hiss will be heard, but it should not be excessive. About $\frac{2}{3}$ rotation will be the normal listening position for the volume control, at which the noise level should be quite unobtrusive. Next, make a recording, perhaps a few sentences of speech. Most people become tongue-tied at this point, so have something handy to read, a newspaper, maker's leaflet or anything. Then, slowly and deliberately, recite the five vowels A, E, I, O, U. Finally shake a bunch of keys, but not too near to the microphone.

Other recorded tests could be made, but there is obviously a practical limit to what you can do as a prospective purchaser! The tests mentioned will give a good indication if one knows what to listen for. On playback the speech should sound natural; listen for distortion and muffling causing lack of clarity. The T and S sounds should be distinct, indicating good transient and high frequency response. Listen at normal level and also at a fairly high level (*not* full volume!) to show up speaker distortions and rattles.

On the vowels, listen for wow and other speed irregularities which show up more on long steady sounds. If in any doubt, try to obtain a tape of some piano music, as this is ideal for revealing wow; it becomes immediately noticeable because the piano (unlike most other instruments) has no tremulo or vibrato effects to disguise it. If the machine has four tracks, the vowel sounds can also be used to check for drop-out, as this is also more detectable with long steady sounds.

The jangling keys are useful for checking the high-frequency response, and can easily be compared with the original sound. If it is a 4-track model, repeat the recordings on the other track (3 if the first test was made on track 1). There is no need to turn the tape over and record all four tracks (or two if a two-track machine) as the same head gaps are used for 2 and 4 as for 1 and 3. Finally, run the tape through the recorded portion with the machine switched to Record and the microphone disconnected or turned right down. This will test the recorder's ability to erase, as there should be no trace of the recording left over the wiped portion of the tape.

All this may seem rather complicated but it is better to find out the faults before buying than afterwards, and if some irregulatities come to

light it will improve one's bargaining position! Actually, no dismantling is involved, other than removing the head cover, and all the tests are
just putting the instrument through its normal functions. If the vendor
seems reluctant to allow such simple tests, then the would-be-buyer
may draw his own conclusions.

## Obsolete Models

One general warning on buying second-hand recorders is worthy of
note. Over the years some makers of tape decks (the mechanisms
minus the case and amplifier) and complete recorders have ceased
producing, so that spare parts are no longer available. Also, spares for
some machines of foreign manufacture may be difficult to find. It is
prudent, therefore, to select a machine of a maker that is currently in
business and advertising a current model. If in doubt ask a dealer; it
can be frustrating to buy a recorder that seems a real bargain and
apparently in good working order, and then to find when a fault occurs,
it is unrepairable.

## Choosing a Microphone

A microphone is usually supplied with each recorder. The small pencil
type with on/off switch that comes with the portable battery machine is
probably the best for the job and quite compatible with the quality
obtainable from such instruments. There is, then, no need to try to
improve things by obtaining a better one for these recorders.

The cheap crystal microphones often supplied with mains-operated
machines leave much to be desired and it is worth investing in
something better. A good moving-coil instrument is the best for
general use, combining good quality with rugged construction. For
best quality a ribbon microphone is the obvious choice, and while
rather more delicate and expensive than other types, there are some
very good models which are no dearer than some of the more expensive
moving-coils. Impedance matching, however, must be considered. If a
crystal microphone was supplied with the recorder, the input will be
high-impedance, requiring either a high-impedance moving-coil or
ribbon model or an in-line transformer for matching.

If the recorder employs transistors and is supplied with a cheap
moving-coil microphone this will be either medium or high-
impedance, and the replacement also must be the same. Some microphones are supplied in dual-impedance form, in which either of two
impedance values can be selected. This is useful where two or more
recorders have different input impedances, as the microphone can be
used with either.

c

It is advantageous to have more than one microphone, especially in the production of tape dramas which involve a number of participants. While some of the old crystal microphones could be pressed into service, it is not a good practice to use different types of microphone at the same time. Each has its characteristic sound, and when used together or in quick succession this quality difference is quite noticeable. Also there are matching difficulties when dissimilar impedances are used (crystals are much higher than even high-impedance moving coils).

### Microphone Mixers

To operate more than one microphone at the same time a mixer unit will be required. This is a device which mixes the signals from several microphones in the proportions needed and feeds them all together into the recorder. The appearance of typical units are shown in Fig. 4.9.

The simplest mixers are passive (i.e. have no amplification) and cost little. With these the output lead must be taken to the microphone socket on the recorder. The main drawback with them is that when a microphone is turned down, the signal is reduced, but the first amplifying stage in the recorder is still operating at high level and therefore generating a certain amount of noise, thus the signal/noise ratio deteriorates.

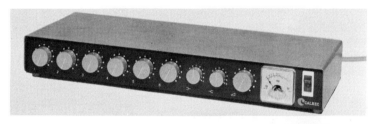

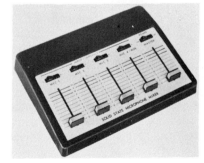

Fig. 4.9 Two types of commercial mixer units. Above—the Calrec model 6MXV which provides mixing facilities for six channels. Right—the Eagle FF1 mixer and preamplifier with four slider type controls plus a master slider to control the total signal output.

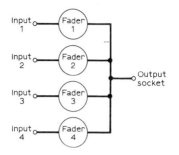

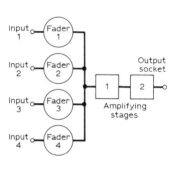

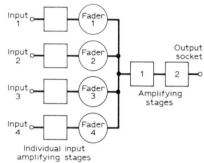

Fig. 4.10 (left) Simplified block diagram of a passive mixer.

Fig. 4.11 (bottom left) Block diagram of amplified mixer with common input amplifying stage.

Fig. 4.12 (bottom right) Block diagram of amplified mixer with individual input stages. The faders reduce the noise generated in the input stages in addition to the microphone signal, thus maintaining a good signal/noise ratio.

Some mixers include transistor amplifying stages run from a small battery, but with most of the lower-priced units, the fader controls are connected across the input sockets, so again the signal from the microphones is reduced while the first amplifying stage operates at high level with maximum noise. If the design of the unit is poor, more noise can result than if a passive mixer were used, because the noise generated by the mixer amplifying circuits is added to that of the recorder first stage.

The best type of mixer has a separate amplifying stage for each input, followed by the fader control. Thus, when the control is turned down, it reduces not only the signal but also the noise of the first stage, and a higher level is then fed to the stages following the faders, where all the signals are combined. Figs. 4.10, 4.11 and 4.12 show simplified block circuit diagrams of the different types.

When an amplified type is used, the output lead should be connected to the tape recorder 'gram' or 'radio input' socket rather than the microphone socket as the latter is designed to handle low-level signals and distortion would result if overloaded.

While amplified types with individual input stages are the best, they are expensive. The amplified mixer with a common input stage confers little advantage, so the simple passive one is probably the most suitable for amatuer recording purposes. The signal/noise ratio will not suffer seriously if the mixer is operated with the faders turned well up (nearly full) and any microphone output which seems too loud in relation to the others eased back a little.

Most mixers have provision for four microphones, ample for most purposes. The output of another tape recorder or record player for music and effects can be fed into the gram socket on the recorder and controlled by the appropriate recorder control, or fed into one of the mixer inputs. The latter will enable all the sound sources to be controlled from one panel, a more convenient arrangement, but the fader will have to be turned well back as the output of a recorder may be far greater than that of a microphone.

### Extension Microphone Lead

An extension microphone lead will be needed to make a recording where it is not convenient to take the recorder or the use of the battery portable recorder is not desired, such as recording effects in the bathroom to obtain a high level of reverberation. About a dozen yards should be enough for most purposes, but it will become a nuisance (and hazard!) if permanently fitted to the microphone.

The extension lead can be made up of screened cable with a single centre conductor, obtainable from most radio dealers. A plug similar to that on the microphone is fitted to one end and a socket, which will receive the microphone plug, to the other. The three types of plug in common use are shown in Fig. 4.13. There are three sizes of jack plug: the standard $\frac{1}{4}$-inch diameter, 3·5mm, and 2·5mm diameters. The standard jack is the most convenient to wire and use and the most reliable because of its large contact surface area. One must, of course, be governed by the type of socket on the recorder.

If you make up the lead yourself, make sure that the metal braiding which constitutes the screening does not make contact with the centre conductor. With all jack plugs, the braiding goes to the body contact of the plug, and the centre conductor to the tip. With the continental type, the braiding is connected to the centre pin of the three and the signal wire to whichever of the other two is used in the particular recorder; check the existing microphone plug to find out. In the case of the phono plug, the centre conductor goes to the centre pin and the braid to the metal skirt. If in any doubt as to the connections or one's ability to fit the plugs, a dealer will probably do the job for a small sum.

|       |       |       |
|-------|-------|-------|
| (a)   | (b)   | (c)   |
| Jack plug | DIN plug | Phono plug |

Fig. 4.13    Three types of plugs in general use. (a) jack plug, (b) Continental (DIN) plug, (c) phono plug.

## Editing Kits

As cutting and editing play an important part in creative tape recording, a tape cutting kit is a necessary accessory. Fortunately, editing kits, even the more sophisticated ones, are not expensive. These are described in more detail in Chapter 6.

These, then are the essential items of equipment. Over the years most recordists accumulate various minor bits and pieces which are useful. The stroboscope mentioned earlier is an inexpensive addition, which can be used to check periodically the speed of the stock recorders, or that of an 'unknown' recorder borrowed for dubbing or copying. A tool for cleaning the heads is also an important item, and more will be said about this in Chapter 13.

CHAPTER FIVE

# RECORDING TECHNIQUES

As THE OLD SONG SAYS: 'It ain't what you do, it's the way that you do it', for while the material or the creative idea is the most important part, it is considerably enhanced or otherwise by the way it is recorded. Some excellent ideas can be spoiled by poor technique; conversely some run-of-the-mill recordings come off very well because of the imaginative way they are recorded.

Good recording techniques must be mastered before any serious attempts at creative recording can be made. They are the finish and polish on the end product. The term 'technique' implies that which is technical and this is true in the case of tape recording. Using our original simile of an artist, he must learn to prepare his canvasses, mix his paints and hold his brushes correctly before exploring what may appear to be the more interesting fields of composition, light-and-shade and perspective.

## Correct Recording Level

Perhaps the first and most elementary requirement is to ensure that the recording level is right. If too low, it can be corrected to some extent by turning up the volume during the playback, but the background noise will also be increased. The result is a continuous hiss which spoils the recording and can even obliterate the quieter parts. When the recording level is too high, all the loud passages are distorted, and in bad cases even those of medium or average volume sound 'edgy' and unpleasant.

All tape recorders have some means of indicating the recording level, except those that are fully automatic. One type is the 'magic-eye' indicator in which a dark segment in a green fluorescent display decreases in width with increasing applied sound, until at overload conditions the segment disappears and the green fluorescent light begins to overlap. A similar indicator used in more recent recorders is the 'magic-ribbon' in which two ribbons of blue light move towards each other as the sound increases, until they touch and overlap. In

either case the maximum level is when the loudest recorded sounds
drive the indicator to just below the overlapping point. Many recorders
now use a VU meter to indicate recording level; this has a mark on the
dial showing the maximum permissible level, beyond which the loudest sounds should not drive the pointer.

## A Dummy Run

There should always be a 'dummy run' (test recording) before the
actual session begins, to check on quality, acoustics and balance (if
more than one signal source is being recorded). It will also afford an
opportunity to find the correct recording level.

It is not always necessary to make an actual recording on tape for
the dummy run. If the recorder is equipped with monitoring facilities
and a lockable pause control, it can be switched to Record and the
pause control engaged. The run can then proceed, with the sounds
being monitored by headphones and the level adjusted by reference to
the modulation indicator.

Remember that the level is dictated by the loudest sounds to be
recorded. The recording may be quiet to start with and later become
louder, which is particularly likely when recording music. A tape-
drama may start off with a quiet conversation while later there may be
a crowd, laughter, ejaculations or raised voices. The dummy run

Fig. 5.1    Sometimes it is convenient to use a tape recorder which has automatic
recording level. This Sony machine features auto/manual recording, operates
from batteries or the mains, has four speeds and an electret (capacitor) built into
the casing.

should include material containing the loudest sounds, and the level set accordingly.

If the piece includes very quiet passages (such as whispering) as well as loud passages, it may be necessary to select two recording levels so that the setting can be altered from one to the other quickly when the need arises without searching for the best one. The alteration should be marked on the control if it is unnumbered, and also on the script. It should be made during a period of silence as otherwise there will be an unnatural increase or decrease of volume. A similar silent part will have to be used after the passage, to restore the level to the previous setting.

## Unnecessary Level Alterations

Any level adjustments, however, should be minor, and serve only to make quiet sounds a little more audible or very loud sounds a little less so. Too much levelling out will sound unreal and could destroy dramatic effect.

There is a further reason for not tampering too much with the level during recording. Every recording location, outdoors, in a studio, or in a room, has its own level of background noise. Put another way, no place is completely free from sound unless it is a specially designed sound-proof room. This noise will be made up of many different components and will be coloured by the acoustics and reverberation pattern of the room or location.

This *ambience* passes unnoticed usually, until it is altered. Thus if a 'silent' recording is made with a live microphone in a room, with no speech or movement, the result may seem to be silence. However, if the microphone is turned down during the recording, the point at which the adjustment was made can be easily detected, because after that point the tape is completely dead.

Because major alterations of the recording level control will affect the ambience, and will be detected, it is preferable to combine minor alterations with changes in microphone usage if a further reduction in dynamic range is required. We will have more to say on this later.

## Starting and Finishing

Pressing the Record key often makes an audible sound which is picked up by the microphone, and electrical surges caused by the switching can produce a click on the recording. It is possible to edit this out later, but it is better to eliminate it from the start. To this end, a recording should be started by engaging the pause control to prevent the tape running, and then switching to Record. If the pause control is then

Fig. 5.2 The modern headphone set is lightweight, comfortable and with cushioned earpads which cut out nearly all ambient noise and simplifies monitoring. Here are two typical examples.

gently released, the recording will get off to a silent start, without clicks or other mechanical noise.

Even so, the start of the recording will seem rather abrupt, because the room ambience and background noises are suddenly heard without warning. A smoother effect will be obtained by starting with the control at zero and then fading it up to the predetermined level decided on during the dummy run. This fade needs to be only a few seconds, but it will make all the difference to the start.

The effect can be heard on public broadcast concerts such as the Proms. We are not pitchforked suddenly into the hall and the commencement of the music without preparation, but there is a slow fade-up of the sounds of the audience and musicians settling down ready for the concert. On these occasions the announcer does not sound as if he were in a sound-proofed control room, but actually in the hall, since the background sounds can be heard behind his voice. This adds enormously to the sense of being present—a valuable lesson for the amateur recordist!

Often the first few words of dialogue in radio plays are faded up, and this also gives a very smooth start. The practice can be applied to tape-dramas providing the first few words are not essential to the plot. Some extra inconsequential lines can be written into the script for the purpose. The ploy is particularly useful where the action starts in the middle of a conversation or speech.

A change of scene or a time interval can also be suggested by fading out, leaving a few seconds blank and then fading up again. Similarly, there can be a fade out at the end, if not during the last words of dialogue, after they have been spoken, in order to 'lose' the ambience of the recording. The tape should then be stopped by the pause control, after which the stop key can be operated; thus clicks and pops at the end of the recording will be avoided.

Let us run over the procedure again. First, a dummy run to check quality, balance and acoustics and to note the correct level of the modulation indicator. Next, turn the control back to zero, engage the pause control and switch to Record. Release the pause control and fade up the level control to the previously noted position, and either during or after this give the signal for the action to commence. Finally, fade out as required, engage pause control and stop.

Broadcast plays should be studied to hear how fades are used. You may have different ideas as to *what* to do, but you can at least learn *how* the professionals do it.

## Exceptions to the Rules

Of course, there are exceptions to the rules. You may wish to achieve a special dramatic effect with an abrupt start or a very long slow fade-up may be required for some special effect. The rules *can* be broken for some specific purpose, if they are first known and understood, but not because of ignorance or negligence.

Just a word here on automatic recorders. These are useful for outdoor or other circumstances where a dummy run may not be possible and it may be impracticable to devote much attention to the level indicator. Those that permit the auto-control to be switched off and the operation to revert to normal manual control are particularly useful, but completely automatic machines with no modulation indicator are of little use for creative recording. It is not possible to perform fades, and the dynamic range is permanently compressed, loud and soft sounds being levelled out; although this may be necessary at times it should be well under the control of the recordist who can use his discretion and judgement as to when it is needed.

## Remote Recordings

Some recordists like to have their recorders remote from the microphones when recording, if possible in a separate room. One reason for this is that any mechanical noise from the recorder, such as motor-whirr or idler-rumble, will not be picked up on the microphones and so appear in the recording.

Another reason is that loudspeaker monitoring can be used. If a loudspeaker is operating in the same volume of air as a microphone and they both are connected to the same amplifier, sounds from the

Fig. 5.3   Although speech recording from a script can be made in the manner shown in the picture, the microphone will pick up noise from the tape recorder and should be placed on a thick pad, suspended from above or used on a floor stand.

loudspeaker will be picked up by the microphone, fed to the amplifier and reproduced again (louder) by the loudspeaker, picked up again by the microphone, amplified, and so on. All this happens in a second or so and the sound can build up into a howl known as acoustic feedback or threshold howl.

It can only be prevented by directing the loudspeaker sound away from the microphone (or keeping the microphone away from the loudspeaker) and by keeping the gain of the amplifier low. Even when the loudspeaker and microphone are at opposite ends of the room and pointing away from each other, if the gain of the amplifier is increased, a point will sooner or later be reached where feedback will take place.

Loudspeaker monitoring in the same room as the microphone is therefore risky; a howl could start by inadvertently increasing the monitor volume control or the microphone control, or by movement of the microphone. Even if feedback did not occur, the loudspeaker would give an echoey effect, which, although useful for special effects, is not desirable for normal recordings.

If a separate room is used, a sound-proof window will be needed to enable the operator to see what is going on and to give the necessary cues. This can lead to practical difficulties. Furthermore, the operator himself may wish to participate in the recording, which he cannot do if he is isolated in another room.

**Recording Nearby**

Headphone monitoring can be better than a loudspeaker because it eliminates outside noise and listening room reverberation. As virtually no sound is radiated from them they can be used quite safely in the same room as the microphone, but if they are removed from the head and placed close to the microphone, feedback could occur.

There is a possibility of mechanical noise from the recorder being picked up by the microphone if it is used close to it or is placed on the same table, as vibrations travel through the wood. Providing they are kept a few feet apart and are not resting on the same piece of furniture, there should be no trouble, as the recorder should be reasonably silent in operation. If it is not, there is a mechanical defect which should be attended to before any serious attempt at creative recording is made. Keeping the microphone and recorder apart should be an adequate precaution and the use of a separate room rarely necessary.

**Room Acoustics**

The effect of room acoustics on the recording can be modified by the way the microphone is used. All enclosed spaces add reverberation to the original sound, the amount and nature depending on the size of the room and the absorbency of the furnishings. Sound will bounce around longer in an empty or sparsely furnished room. A lot of wooden furniture will absorb some of the sound and so reduce the reverberation fairly evenly over the normal speech frequency range. A lot of upholstery, carpeting and curtains will absorb most of the high frequencies but will affect the lower frequencies much less.

Speech needs a certain amount of reverberation to make it crisp and pleasing to listen to. Without any, it sounds thin and lifeless, but with too much it becomes unintelligible, as the words and syllables run into each other. A large empty room would almost certainly have too much reverberation unless it was needed for a special effect. On the other hand one furnished with a lot of heavy upholstery and carpeting with underfelt, will sound dead and muffled. The ideal lies between the two.

A fair amount of wooden furniture, average curtaining, one or two upholstered chairs and thin carpeting (or none at all) should give good acoustics for normal speech. This is the condition usually found in the average dining room, and recordings will have a livelier, more pleasing, sound than those made in the lounge.

It is recommended that trial recordings of speech be made in each of the available rooms in the house. This will demonstrate the effect of the different acoustics (sometimes to a surprising degree), will reveal the

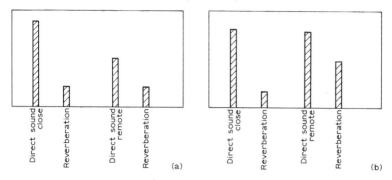

Fig. 5.4 (a) Comparative levels of direct sound picked up close to the microphone with room reverberation, and direct sound remote from the microphone with the same level of reverberation. (b) Increasing the level of remote sound to that of near sound by turning up the modulation control also increases reverberation level proportionately. Thus, there is more reverberation when the sound source is remote from the microphone.

best conditions for general speech recording, and suggest the use of different rooms for different effects.

### Reverberation and Microphone Distance

The amount of direct sound picked up by a microphone depends on the distance between it and the sound source. Reverberation, on the other hand, will be fairly constant whatever the microphone position, because it is coming in from all angles. It follows, then, that the ratio of direct sound to reverberation can be varied by altering the microphone distance.

Speaking close to the microphone requires that the recording level control will have to be turned down because of the high sound-level, thus reducing the level of reverberation. However, when speaking further away from the microphone, the direct sound is much less and the control must be turned up to compensate, and this raises the proportion of reverberation.

Fig. 5.4 (a) shows the comparison between the direct sound pickup of a close and remote microphone. The reverberation levels are the same in both cases. At (b) we have the two recording levels with the direct sound inputs made equal by adjustment of the microphone control. As the levels of the reverberation are proportionately altered, it can be seen that there is more reverberation with the remote microphone than with the close one.

This effect can be used to modify the reverberation characteristics of the recording room. For most normal applications a microphone distance of about 12 inches is usual. However, where room reverberation is excessive, a rather closer position will reduce it; and where it is insufficient a more distant position will increase it. It should be noted that in the latter case, a satisfactory increase in reverberation will only be achieved where the reverberation characteristic of the room is fairly even over the frequency range.

If, for example, the room is acoustically dead because of a preponderance of heavy carpeting and upholstery, it will be highly absorbent of the higher frequencies. Increasing the microphone distance will increase reverberation mainly of the lower frequencies as these are the only ones being reflected back. Even the higher frequencies of the direct sound may suffer absorption before reaching the microphone. The net effect will be to make the speech sound even more muffled and indistinct.

Fig. 5.5 This unusual microphone made by Grundig incorporates a built-in reverberation amplifier which runs from a small battery.

### Simulating Outdoor Recordings

When recording tape dramas, the acoustic characteristic of the recording room must be taken into account, and modified if required. If, for example, the action is supposed to be taking place in the open air, there should be no reverberation at all. The 'dead' room, then, shunned for ordinary recordings, would be ideal for simulating outdoor scenes.

Consideration may be given to the idea of recording such sequences actually in the open air to get the right acoustic effect, but this is fraught with snags. Sounds that are not heard, or pass unnoticed by the human ear, have an unhappy knack of being rendered prominent by the microphone. Thus, the sounds of distant traffic, children playing, or a dog barking streets away, can all be faithfully captured, although not noticed at the time. If the scene is supposed to be in the middle of the Sahara desert, the result can hardly be described as realistic!

There is also the possibility of wind noise on the microphone. Even a gentle breeze can produce roaring and fluttering sounds caused by air turbulence around the microphone casing and blowing the diaphragm or ribbon back and forth. Ribbon microphones are rather prone to this because of the lightness of the ribbon. Wind-shields can be used to partly overcome this, but unless designed for the particular microphone the cure is only partial. Outdoor recording, then, unless of special location sequences, creates more problems than it solves, and it is better to try to achieve a dead acoustic indoors.

Even indoors there can be problems from extraneous noises, especially if near a main road, or if the walls are thin and the neighbours are hi-fi enthusiasts. Using a room furthest from the source of noise is an obvious first step. Drawing heavy curtains across the windows will help reduce outside noise. Choosing an off-peak traffic time for recording can also help. Another tip is to disconnect the door bell and take the telephone off the hook before starting a recording session!

**Adjusting Acoustics**

Other changes in the acoustics may be required, according to the nature of the subject. A domestic sequence in a back-parlour would need a moderate reverberation; a closer microphone placing would give this, and add the intimacy needed for such a scene. If the local pub is the setting, rather more reverberation would be needed because of the large size and absence of heavy furnishings; this could be obtained by a wider microphone spacing or the choice of a more reverberant room. A speech in the village hall could be simulated by placing the microphone several feet from the actor, giving more reverberation and a more distant effect.

In each case the actors would need to adjust their volume to suit the location. In domestic scenes, the tone would be conversational and subdued, unless an argument was scripted! For the pub, conversational again, but heightened somewhat to overcome the background sounds (more on this subject in a later chapter). For the speech, the actor would need to raise his voice as though he were actually addressing a large gathering.

A highly reverberant setting such as a swimming bath, underground cavern, or cathedral, is difficult to simulate without the use of an echo chamber or reverberation unit. The latter produces artificial reverberation by passing sound vibrations along a pair of steel springs; good ones are very effective but the cheap versions do not provide very good quality and realism.

Reasonable results can be obtained by using a tiled bathroom, especially if curtains and towels are removed. Face the microphone into one corner, a couple of feet away, and have the actors speak into the opposite corner. Another dodge is to mount the microphone in the bath (without any water!). It is very worthwhile experimenting to find the best position, and it gives more satisfaction to get good results by improvising with resources to hand than by using expensive and elaborate equipment to obtain the same ends. However, good equipment should not be spurned if it is available, for there is no virtue in making things deliberately difficult!

Just a general point on microphone distance. The actors or speakers should be instructed to vary their distance or speaking angle according to volume level. Thus for a shout or ejaculation, the head should be moved back and turned slightly away from the microphone. When the voice has to be dropped, or a whisper produced, the head can be moved toward the microphone. This will minimise control adjustments which can sometimes be detected in the recording. Otherwise distance should be maintained to avoid volume fluctuations.

**Mounting the Microphone**

It is important that microphones are supported, to avoid vibration or knocks which would make themselves heard in the recording. Generally, they should not be held in the hand, although in some cases this may be unavoidable. Noise can result due to rubbing or unconcious 'playing' with the microphone or lead, and during a lengthy session the hand can wander from its original position, giving a different volume and also a different acoustic characteristic.

If the instrument must be hand-held, it should be of the stick type, and held rigidly in the same position. With dialogues or interviews, the microphone should be inclined slightly to one person, then to the other as each one speaks. This should not be too pronounced otherwise words may be lost if someone speaks too soon or adds an afterthought after the microphone has been pointed away. A lesser movement of the microphone will catch something, at least, if one speaks out of turn.

A table stand is useful for normal indoor recording as it can be adjusted for height and position relative to the speakers. It is good practice to place the stand on a pad of felt or foam rubber so that any

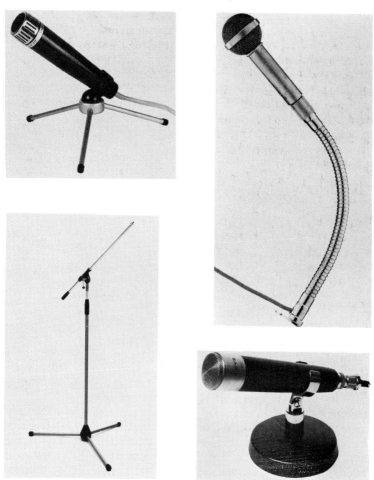

Fig. 5.6   Typical examples of table stands, a floor stand and a swan-neck fitting.

jolting of the table will not be transmitted up the stand to the micro-phone. If several people are seated around a table it is more than likely that someone will kick one of the legs or strike it with his hand. This may pass unnoticed at the time but would spoil an otherwise good recording.

The safest support from the viewpoint of isolation from vibration or shock is to suspend the microphone from the ceiling. A stick microphone will need to be angled sideways so that the end is pointing towards the actors as if it were on a stand. This calls for two suspension cords, but one of these can be the microphone cable itself. A cord tied to the other end will lift it to a sideways position. Both cord and cable can be supported from a single point such as a light fitting, but there is sometimes a tendency for the microphone to rotate and face the wrong way. A more stable arrangement is to find two different fixing points, such as a light fitting in the centre of the ceiling and a point at the top of one of the walls (Fig. 5.7).

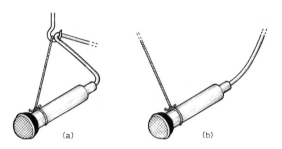

Fig. 5.7    A microphone suspended from a single fixing point (a) and from two points (b).

## Multiple Situations

One microphone can be used by up to three persons, but in the case of three the distance should be greater than usual so that all will be facing the front of the instrument. Remember that there is very little pickup from any microphone at its side. Sensitivity decreases as the angle from the front increases, reaching its minimum at the side, but the area of lower sensitivity can be used by placing speakers at the side nearer than any in front, thereby obtaining an equal volume to all (Fig. 5.8). It may be possible to arrange four in similar manner, but the distance between them and the microphone must be increased further, but this will have the effect of introducing more room reverberation.

For four (or even three) persons it is better to use two microphones. They should be of similar type because each type has its own characteristic response and if two dissimilar ones are used together the difference is quite noticeable. One microphone to two persons permits a closer spacing and so a greater control over the room accoustics. It is not advisable to have a group of people around a single microphone, each one using it at his or her cue. This can introduce unwanted noises of movement, unnatural delays in the dialogue and it will be difficult to keep the levels constant with so many position changes.

If more than one microphone is to be used, a mixer will be required. If it is one with no amplification, make sure that the controls are turned well up as a low setting will decrease the signal-to-noise ratio. About three-quarters is a good starting position for all controls on the mixer

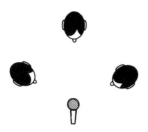

Fig. 5.8    In this diagram showing three actors around a single microphone, note that those at the side are placed a little nearer to allow for the reduced microphone pickup at that angle.

that are in use. This permits any to be turned up a little more if required to get a balance. If the balance is good with the controls in the same position, then they can all be turned to maximum to get the best signal-to-noise performance. Fading can be done from the level control on the tape recorder.

## Multiple Microphones for Music

Live music can pose many problems. If there are a number of instrumentalists, one method is to provide a microphone for each one or for each section; the mixer controls can then be adjusted to get a good balance between them. In order that each microphone should pick up only its own instrument (which is necessary if it is required to fade the others down), a close microphone position is necessary.

This arrangement is usually the best for public performances that are amplified, because the loudspeakers are in the same hall as the microphones and feedback would occur if too much amplification were used. A close microphone position gives a high output from the microphone and therefore there is less need for amplification from the amplifier. It is also often used in recording studios to get a clear incisive recording of each instrument, and so that special effects such as reverberation or echo can be added to any instrument.

For straight recording, however, it is not necessarily the best. Balance is not easy to achieve, musical instruments are louder and more penetrating than speech and when monitoring (even with head-phones) the instruments can be heard directly, which makes it difficult to assess the balance coming over the phones. This is one case where a separate sound-proof room would be an asset.

Furthermore, the control settings can be quite critical for ideal balance. If one is just too low or too high, one instrument will either overshadow the others or be scarcely heard. Errors of this nature with speech are not so bad in their effect because we do not have everyone talking at once! A further point is that the blending of the instruments is not so good; we are more conscious of the individual instruments than the total effect.

### Single Microphone Technique

As a general rule, better results can be obtained by using just a single microphone placed strategically to pick up all the instruments. Balance is achieved by placing the various performers at different distances from the microphone, the loud ones such as the brass at the rear, woodwind intermediate, and strings at the front. A piano can be placed to the side, providing the sounding board is facing the microphone. Upright pianos should have their lid open and angled toward the microphone. If there is some loss of clarity, the piano should be given a separate microphone, directed into the instrument a little to the right (towards the treble) of centre.

By using a single microphone, errors of balance are not so likely once the positioning is worked out and a few test recordings made to check and modify the placings. A better blending of the instruments results because there is more reverberation and this will be made up of reflected sound from all the instruments. This additional reverberation is an advantage because music needs more reverberation than speech.

As in the case of the piano, there may be some performers who need their own microphone because of their instrument being particularly soft or difficult to pick out from the others. Instruments such as the glockenspiel would come in this class. Vocalists would also need their own microphone, otherwise they may be overshadowed by the accom-panying music, and may sound distant in the recording because of excessive reverberation due to the more remote microphone position.

### Experiment for Best Results

Although these general principles will hold good in most cases, success with any particular recording of live music will come only by experi-menting with different positions. Do not be afraid to make quite a number of short test recordings in order to get the best results.

Experiment, too, is the only way to discover the best microphone technique for other types of sound, for each one must be handled differently. A rule worth remembering is to keep the microphone out of any air stream that may be caused by the sound source. Thus, a jet-aircraft taking off is better recorded from a distance, and a fast moving train recorded well out of the slip-stream. Wind instruments should not be pointed with their flares directly at the microphone.

Electric fans and vacuum cleaners can be used to simulate various effects, but again the microphone must be kept out of the actual flow of air. Failure to do this will give the same effect as wind noise when recording in the open air, and will obliterate the actual sound.

## Copying via Loudspeaker

Copying, dubbing and mixing of recordings all have applications in creative recording. Copying, for instance, may be needed for making complete duplicates of recordings or for copying sections of a recording for inclusion into another without damaging the original. Copies are sometimes made by standing a microphone of the copying recorder in front of the loudspeaker of the playing one. This is a bad practice because the greatest amount of distortion in a tape recorder is generated in the loudspeaker and the output stage that drives it; the microphone can also add distortion, and it certainly modifies the frequency response of material passing through it.

There will also be reverberation and absorption of various frequencies due to the acoustics of the room in which the copy is made, and also mechanical noise from the playing recorder (the microphone picking up sound directly from it). In addition there is the possibility of random sounds being made in or outside the room while the copying is going on, and these too will be added to the copy.

## Direct Lead Copying

Most tape recorders of good design include a socket from which the signal can be tapped off before it is applied to the output stage and loudspeaker. It may be labelled 'Line', 'Tape Out', 'Amplifier' or something similar. If a lead with a suitable plug is fitted to this socket and the other end plugged into the auxiliary or gram socket of the copying recorder, a first-class copy can be made without using a microphone or the loudspeaker circuits of the playing recorder, and without the acoustics or noises in the room having any effect (Fig. 5.9).

In making the copy, the same procedure should be adopted as for making a live recording. First make a test recording to set the modulation level, then hold on the pause controls with one recorder switched to Record and the other to Playback. Release the pause control of the copying machine and fade up the level control to the predetermined position, and then release the pause control of the playback machine and fade up the volume control to its position. See that the recorded material does not start immediately on the original otherwise the fade up will cut into it. Load the tape so that there is about a foot of tape or leader in advance of the actual start to allow for this.

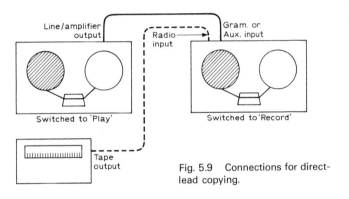

Fig. 5.9    Connections for direct-lead copying.

If both machines are 3-speed models and the original recording is at one of the lower speeds, the copying can be done at the highest speed. The frequency response may undergo slight modification by doing this, but the wow and flutter performance will be better, as speed stability increases with tape speed and the copy may be somewhat better for being made at the higher speed. There is also the convenience of completing the copy in half the time that it would take at its normal speed.

**Superimposing**

The simplest method of superimposing one recording on another is by running the first recording through the machine with the erase head disconnected and recording over the original. Some recorders have a switch for turning the erase head off for this purpose, but usually these switches have to be held in position as a protection against accidental non-erasure should they be inadvertently left in the 'off' position.

In practice this is inconvenient because one hand is engaged during superimposing; in an attempt to make their machines mistake-proof, the makers have lessened the usefulness of this facility. If you can devise some means of holding the switch in position, then do so, but ensure that when making normal recordings the switch is in the 'on' position otherwise the maker's argument will be justified!

There are limitations in this method. When a second recording is made over the first one, it is partially erased by the bias in the recording head. As we cannot dispense with the bias, this effect cannot be avoided. The result is that there is a drop in volume of the original and also the higher frequencies are curtailed as these are erased more than lower ones.

Because of this, it is desirable to put the less important recording on the tape first. For example, to add background music to a speech commentary, tape the music first; similarly sound effects should be put on before the main programme. The second recording must start before the first one, and end after it, so that it overlaps it at both ends. This must be done even if the second one is intended to be shorter, as for example when background music extends after the commentary has finished. If this is the case, the second recording must be continued

Fig. 5.10 This photograph showing copying from one recorder to another by direct lead looks perfectly correct but in actual fact distortion would result because the lead to the copying machine is plugged into the microphone socket instead of the auxiliary socket and would thereby overload the input stage.

with the microphone turned off so that the partial erasing action continues to beyond the end of the first recording.

The reason for this is that if the second recording stops short of the end of the first one, or starts after it, there will be a noticeable change in the quality at that point. An exception could be made, however, to obtain a special effect such as an increase in volume and clarity of the closing bars of background music at the end of a commentary.

Another limitation is that the two recordings cannot easily be synchronised. All we hear in the monitor is the second recording which is passing through the recorder amplifier, with no means of knowing the contents of the first one already on tape. Some machines have a monitor that picks up what is actually on the tape, i.e., they have separate record and playback heads, permitting the operator to hear both recordings together. Users of less sophisticated machines must devise other means of synchronising.

The best method is to time the main programme, noting where music or effects must be added. Then run a blank tape through the recorder and time it from the beginning, putting on the music and effects at the right times. Next, key the back of the tape by sticking on some coloured tape or marking with a Chinagraph (wax) pencil where the effects occur and at one minute beforehand. Make the main recording over the effects recording, using the key marks as a guide to timing. The one minute warning will indicate if the script is running fast or slow, by comparing with a one-minute cue mark on the script.

From this it may seem that as superimposing involves some 'fiddling' in getting the timing right, and one of the two recordings is degraded in quality, it is of dubious worth. There are, however, better methods of getting the same results, but these need either three recorders or two pairs of hands for operating, or both. The dubbing method needs only two recorders and it can be managed single-handed, so it has some redeeming features.

With a machine having no erase switch, it is possible to dub by devising some means of holding the tape away from the erase head and this will depend on the layout of the machine and materials to hand. Whatever is used should be non-magnetic and not likely to damage the head-face, so do not stick anything (e.g. Sellotape) to the head-face, as the sticky deposit may later cause speed fluctuation. The device should be secure and not likely to become displaced, as it may cause a jam, or the tape could be erased, without the operator knowing it (Fig. 5.11).

A neat and convenient method is to cut a piece of hard plastics material to the height of the head, but wider, warm it so that it becomes soft but not sticky, then apply it to the head face and wrap the edges around the sides. It will take on the contour of the head, will stay in place, and can be removed and refitted easily as desired. Of course, a

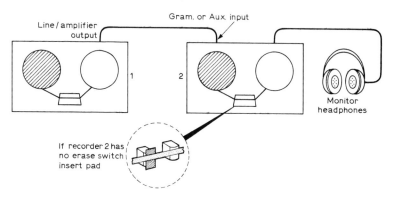

Fig. 5.11   When superimposing, if the second recorder has no switch for disconnecting the erase head, a pad must be inserted (see text).

switch could be fitted somewhere convenient on the deck (the head cover is the easist place usually) to interrupt the lead to the erase head. If doubtful as to ones ability to do this, a local dealer may do the job for a small charge.

## Mixing-in Effects

Another method of adding music or effects is to mix them in at the time of the main recording. A second recorder is set up. A tape containing the music or effects is played from one recorder to another in the same way as for making a copy. This will be controlled by the auxiliary or gram control on the recorder, and the microphone by its own control.

Normally, the level controls are adjusted so that peak sounds give the maximum reading on the modulation indicator. This still applies to the microphone signals but *not* with the added effects; such levels would be far too high and instead of being in the background they would compete with and even over-ride the main programme. It is a common mistake to have the effects too loud, but with superimposing it is not so likely, because the superimposed recording always dominates due to partially erasing the previous recording.

The best balance must be sought by test recording and careful monitoring during the actual recording. If the effect is continuous (such as a car or train journey) it can be louder to start with to establish what it is, then gradually faded to a lower level as the scene proceeds, leaving it unobtrusively in the background. It can be faded up during pauses in the action to indicate passage of time, and then back again for the next sequence. Some effects need to dominate, because of their nature, such as an explosion or street accident. These are of short duration and as there will be no dialogue at the same time, they can be allowed to fully modulate the tape.

When mixing in from another recording in this manner, there is plenty to occupy the attention. If more than one microphone is being used, the mixer must be adjusted, then the main microphone control and the effects control operated while monitoring for balance and quality. In addition to this, the effects recorder must be switched on and the pause control released when required, and its volume control set to give the needed signal. The tape must be watched to see that the effect or music does not overrun. Similarly if the effect or music is on disc, the gram-unit must be operated and the pickup set down at the required position and watched to see it does not overrun.

Really, this is rather a lot for one pair of hands and eyes, and although it is possible to manage it, the operator is working under pressure, and so errors of balance or cueing can easily occur. It is preferable to have an assistant who can attend to the other recorder or gram-unit. Give him the cue to start a few seconds before the effect is required so that you can fade up on your control. Sudden effects such as the explosion or street accident cannot be faded up, of course, and must be set up on a second recorder to start almost immediately the pause button is released (allowing about half-a-second for the tape to get up speed) and then brought in exactly on cue.

### Post Recording Mixing

An easier way of adding extra sounds requires the use of three recorders. The main recording is played on one machine and the effects on another, both being mixed into and recorded by a third. In this way, mistakes will not spoil the main recording and another attempt can be made. When combining the output of two recorders in this way it is not satisfactory to feed one into the gram input and the other into the microphone input, as the latter will be overloaded by the high-level signal and will distort. Use a microphone mixer, preferably one without amplification otherwise it, too, may overload.

If a mixer is not available, the outputs of the two recorders can be combined and fed into the single gram input socket on the third recorder. The simplest way of doing this is to make up a double jumper-lead (Fig. 5.12a). Two screened cables are connected in parallel into one plug, and plugs are fitted to their other ends. Jack-plugs are shown in the illustration but any type of plug, to suit the recorders, can be fitted. To use, one plug is fitted to the gram input socket of the third recorder, and the other two to the output sockets of the two playing recorders. Balance is adjusted by operating the respective volume controls on the playing recorders.

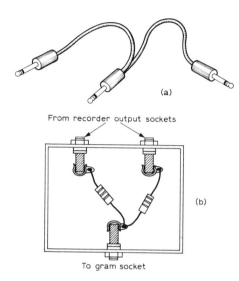

Fig. 5.12    (a) Double jumper lead to mix the output of two recorders into a single input socket. (b) Junction box with isolating resistors to combine two outputs where the recorders have different output impedances. The resistors are 47kΩ each.

It can happen that paralleling the outputs of the two recorders causes interaction between them, especially if one is a transistor and the other a valve machine. To overcome this, an isolating resistor should be wired in series with each output lead, using a small metal box with appropriate sockets to house the circuit (Fig. 5.12b). Normally, audio sockets are made so that one pole is earthed to the metalwork supporting it. There are certain plastics jack sockets that are insulated from their support. Connection must therefore be made to the box, from each of the sockets, from the terminal that contacts the body of the plug. Failure to do this will result in hum.

### Sound-with-Sound

Some 4-track recorders have what is known as *duo-play* or *sound-with-sound* facilities. This enables the procedure described for three recorders to be carried out on two. The main recording is made on track 1. Then, while listening to this recording, the effects are recorded on track

3. Then, both tracks are played simultaneously by operating the parallel-track switch on the recorder, and the result fed into another recorder to combine them into a single recording. If the effects recording is unsatisfactory, it can be erased without disturbing the main recording on track 1. On some machines it will not be possible to listen to both tracks while recording the effects, in which case balancing will be a matter of guesswork and trial-and-error.

In this chapter, we have described some of the basic techniques for recording. Others, dealing with specific applications, will be described in later chapters.

# CHAPTER SIX

# EDITING

IT MAY BE THOUGHT that all the skilled technique and creative work goes into the planning, preparation and recording of the tape, and that once the 'Stop' key has been pressed, the job is finished. This is not the case. The success of the project depends on the subsequent editing; good material can often be rendered ineffective by poor editing, and second-rate material can be greatly improved by imaginative editing.

Editing involves cutting the tape, eliminating the superfluous or the mistakes, re-arranging parts into a different order, including parts of other recordings and generally tidying up. The thought of cutting a tape is often frightening to the beginner, and few seem inclined to take the step, but a well-made joint can be easily and safely made, and is certainly worthwhile if it improves the recording.

Not all recordings need editing; simple and comparatively straightforward tapes may turn out as planned and require no further attention. The creative recordist, however, will usually have afterthoughts, or note places where improvements can be made when hearing the first playback.

## Wet Jointing

Cutting and splicing can be divided into the 'dry' and 'wet' methods. The wet method is most favoured by professionals because it is considered to make the stronger joint, although it is more tricky. A vertical cut is made in the tape and the coating cleaned off at one end to expose the tape material. Solvent is applied and the two ends brought together to form an overlap joint. The result is a strong welding of the two parts. However, if too much solvent is applied, especially on a thin tape, it can weaken it because it softens and partly dissolves the tape material. If too little is used the result will be an incomplete weld which will be weak.

The overlap must exactly occupy the cleaned off space otherwise there will be a gap in the coating and subsequent recordings made on the tape will suffer from a momentary break in sound. If on the other hand the overlap goes beyond the area of cleaned-off tape, the edge of the joint will not 'take', and may curl back. Precision jointing blocks help to make things easier, but a good deal of skill and experience is needed to make perfect joints by this method.

## Dry Jointing

In the dry method, a diagonal cut is first made across the tape. When a diagonal cut passes the vertical head-gap it does so gradually as shown in Fig. 6.1 and there is always a portion of both parts of the tape across the head-gap, providing a smooth transition from one to the other. Any magnetic disturbance at the edge caused by the cutting will be evened out; similarly any loss of coating in the cutting will have a minimal effect because there will still be a large area of magnetic material in contact with the gap.

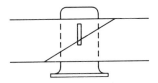

Fig. 6.1    When a diagonal join posses over the vertical head gap, part of both sections are always crossing it at the same time, thus making the passage smooth and noise free.

Jointing blocks are available having a guide for making the cuts, so that all will be at the same angle and therefore will marry with any other cut. Some blocks have a built-in blade which makes the cut, while others need an external cutter. Non-magnetic scissors are sometimes provided for the purpose but the use of these involves marking the tape along the guide groove, and then lifting it out of the block to cut it. A sharp razor blade is the easiest to use as the cut can be made along the guide groove without marking the tape or moving it from the block.

The purpose of a non-magnetic blade is to eliminate the possibility of magnetising the tape at the cut and thus producing a click as the joint passes the head. An ordinary steel blade need not become magnetised to the extent of making a noisy joint (in any case, the diagonal cut should take care of it) but it is very important to make a good clean cut. Non-magnetic blades are softer than steel and dull more quickly, hence they are not so likely to give a clean cut.

In making the joint, the two ends are brought together so that they meet but do not overlap. A channel in the jointing block, cut to exactly the width of the tape, ensures that the two ends of the tape are in line. Some blocks have clamps that secure the tape while the splicing is carried out.

The splicing tape is then secured to the back of the tape, overlapping the cut by about half-an-inch either side; only tape specially made for the purpose should be used as other forms of adhesive tape sometimes stretch, shrink, or deform, and thus put the joint out of alignment. Another factor is that the adhesive used with many tapes is of a general-purpose nature and is inclined to be rather soft, after a time tending to migrate to the edges, and thus the adjacent layer of recording tape becomes stuck to it. The joint also tends to get stuck in the tape guides for the same reason.

## Splicing Tapes

Various widths of splicing tape up to half-an-inch are available. Those that are wider than the recording tape require less precision in application and can be trimmed to size with a pair of scissors. Splicing tape must not overlap the recording tape by even a small amount. Tape guides on recorders are accurately made to the size of the recording tape to ensure that the tracks register correctly with the head gap. An overlap of splicing tape will increase the tape width and cause it to become jammed in the guides. Furthermore, the exposed adhesive surface is a hazard to the adjacent layer.

It is, therefore, normal practice to cut-in slightly when trimming as in Fig. 6.2, shown exaggerated for clarity. If carefully confined to a slight

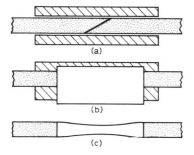

Fig. 6.2   (a) First step in making the joint—making a diagonal cut across both ends with the tape held in place in a jointing block. (b) Applying a strip of splicing tape. (c) Surplus cut off and the edges undercut (shown exaggerated) to ensure that the splicing tape does not overlap the recording tape and leave any adhesive surface exposed.

'shaving', no harm will come to the recording because the tracks do not extend right to the edge of the tape. Some splicers are available, however, which take care of all these factors. In addition to a splicing block with tape guide and clamps, these splicers incorporate a sliding double-cutter with a Cut position for making the diagonal joints and a Trim position for removing excess splicing tape and making the undercut in one action.

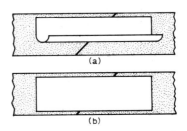

Fig. 6.3    (a) When using $\frac{7}{32}''$ splicing tape apply top edge first, leaving it just short of the edge of the recording tape. (b) Press down into place; no cutting in is required.

Editing cassette tapes is a more tricky operation, but a kit is now available to enable these tapes to be easily, quickly and accurately edited. The kit comprises tape splicer, two cutters, tape piercer, splicing tape and other accessories and contains full instructions for use.

**What to Cut Out**

One obvious purpose of tape editing is to get rid of unwanted noises such as coughs, objects being kicked or dropped, and so on. Clicks due to making a start without using the pause control can also be edited out. The first step is to mark the section of the tape to be removed. The tape speed will give a rough guide as to how much to cut out; thus at $3\frac{3}{4}$i/s, a two-second interval will mean a tape length of $7\frac{1}{2}$ inches.

Play the tape over where the unwanted part is recorded and determine the margin of silence either side of the sound. If, say, a cough occurs between successive sentences in a dialogue, care would have to be taken not to cut part of the speech before and after the cough. Hence the cut would have to be taken right up to the start of the cough and immediately it had ceased. If, however, it occurs during a natural pause and there is silence before and after, the cutting will not be so critical.

The best way to find the precise section, is to stop the tape just before the unwanted sound, by means of the pause control. Then turn the take-up spool by hand slowly to find the start of the unwanted

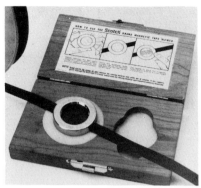

Fig. 6.4 (left) A tape editing kit comprising tape splicer, tape reel labels, razor cutter, splicing tape and tape marker (Bib Division, Multicore Solders).

Fig. 6.5 (right) It can be useful to the keen tape recordist to view the recorded tracks. This can be done with this tape viewer. (3M Company).

sound. Despite the much lower pitch, due to the slow speed of tape past the head, it should be possible to recognise it and make an exact 'fix' of its position.

The part of the tape to be marked is now lying immediately across the record/playback head, and if the slot in the recorder is wide enough, the tape can be marked *in situ* with a Chinagraph pencil or (if there is no room to manoeuvre one in the space) a sliver of splicing-tape can be introduced with a pair of tweezers and stuck on to the tape. Because of the pressure pad, it cannot be placed directly on the spot, but sticking it to the right of the pad will give a small margin just before the commencement of the sound.

With some machines, there is not even room to insert a pair of tweezers, and it will be necessary to accurately measure beforehand the distance from the head to the right-hand tape-guide at the end of the slot. This measurement can be marked off at some convenient position on the tape deck. Having found the start of the sound, put a marker temporarily on the tape that is across the guide, remove the tape from the slot, and measure back the required length from the marker. Put a new marker here and remove the old one.

Next, find the exact position for the end of the sound in the same way. There may be some reverberation or other after-sound effects, so if the material which follows permits, take the marker a little beyond the apparent end of the sound; about an inch should do. With the section marked, cut it out, make diagonal cuts at the ends with the aid of the splicing block and join up. Of course, it is not only unwanted

D

sound that can be eliminated in this way. Excessive pauses slow up the
action and these too can be cut out, the process being less critical. All
that is needed here is to determine the length by which the pause must
be shortened, and cut out the appropriate section in the middle of the
pause. Accurate marking is not required.

### Disguising the Break

There are certain points to watch when removing sections of tape.
Having eliminated the undesired sound we have also upset the timing.
Taking a cough, our previous example, the speech before and after will
now follow without a break, and unless there was a certain pause at the
time of the recording, this may sound rather unnatural. If so, it may be
necessary to insert an inch or two of blank tape in order to provide a
pause. The snag now is that the blank section will be dead, without any
room ambience, and this may be noticeable.

Being in the middle of dialogue it may pass unnoticed and is not so
bad as having an abrupt unfaded-in start at the beginning of the
recording. However, it is one of those minor details which distinguish a
professional sounding recording from an ordinary amateur effort. The
remedy is quite simple. Record a couple of minutes of 'silence' at the
end of the actual recording in the recording room with the microphones turned on; this tape can then be used if required for providing
any such pauses.

Another difficulty may arise if there is any background sound-effect
added at the time of recording. There is no problem if this is of a
formless nature such as rain, crowd noise and the like, but where there
is some form or rhythm to the effect such as the slow ticking of a
grandfather clock, the sound of oars, footsteps or worse still, music, a
section cut out will obviously play havoc with these.

To facilitate editing, it will help to add such effects after the
recording has been made, as outlined in the previous chapter. Whether to
add later or mix in at the time depends on the type and amount of effect.
If only a short passage is involved, mixing at the time could be risked,
as it may not be necessary to edit in that section, but if a fairly long
passage of rhythmic sound is to be added, it would be better to do it
after the main recording to avoid tricky editing.

### Interpolating and Rearranging

Removing unwanted passages is not the only reason for editing; it may
be desired to splice in part of another recording. To do this, make a cut
in the tape at the point where the extra material is to be inserted, and
join in the new section. Two joints are required: one at the beginning

and one at the end of the interpolation. When the extra tape is cut ready to splice in, mark the beginning with a Chinagraph pencil or piece of splicing tape as it is very easy to put the tape in the wrong way round.

Quite complicated editing involving the re-arrangement of sections of the recording is not only possible but sometimes necessary. This calls for an orderly method to be applied if a hopeless muddle is not to be the result. The first step is to draw up a written list or description of the tape, the individual sections being numbered for identification. Next, prepare a new list showing the revised order and giving numerical identification. Note also where it is required to insert pauses, shorten sections, etc.

The sections should now be identified on the tape and marked, then cut. As the chances of mixing them up are considerable, each section should be marked with its number. Additionally, it will be necessary to mark the beginning of each portion, because with several cut lengths it is almost certain that at least one will be put in the wrong way if they are unmarked. This can be easily done by marking the beginning

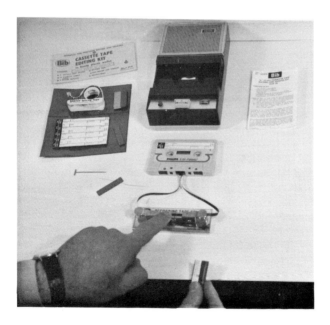

Fig. 6.6   A complete kit for editing cassette tapes, comprising tape splicer, tape cutters, tape piercer, self-adhesive cassette and container labels, splicing tape, tape winders and removers. (Bib Division, Multicore Solders).

with the numerical section identification, thus killing two birds with one stone.

How the tape lengths are stored while the joining up process is being conducted depends rather on their length. If they are just a few feet long, the best arrangement is to hang them over some horizontal object such as a curtain rail, in an elevated position. Then each one can be identified by its mark, pulled off and spliced in as required. With longer sections it is better to wind them on small reels, with the beginning on the outside so that it can be joined in place without first having to unreel it. When the joint is made it can be wound with the rest onto the master reel, and the next section joined to its tail, and so on until all are used up.

A supply of 3-inch reels is very useful for editing in this way. A ciné enthusiast friend may have some spare film-reels; when 50-foot runs of 8mm film are returned from the processors, they are wound on 3-inch spools, and since most enthusiasts join these up to make longer films they may accumulate a number of small spools that are not required.

## Trick Effects

Trick effects can be obtained by careful editing. It is, for example, possible to rearrange words in a speech or conversation so that a completely different meaning is given. While this is an interesting exercise in editing and can be fun, the ethical dangers are obvious, which is why courts of law regard recorded evidence with suspicion. Often, though, the trick is given away by unnatural voice inflexions. Another trick is to record a short piece by a normally well-spoken person and then remove all the H's, but such ideas are more in the realm of party-tricks than creative recording.

A practice which has more creative possibilities is to remove the beginning or ends of certain sounds, which can completely change their character, especially those of some musical instruments. This can be a fruitful source when looking for unusual sounds for musique concrete sequences. More of this, however, in later chapters.

## Condensing

A recording must sometimes be reduced in length for competition or broadcast purposes, and it is often quite difficult to decide what to cut out or shorten for it seems that to interfere with any part will spoil it, yet a condensation must be made. However, if a copy is made of the original, a later comparison between the two will often show the recordist to his surprise that the cut-down version is better.

This is perhaps not so surprising on reflection. In making the condensation all non-essential material is eliminated, leaving only the cream. Pauses which may have been a trifle overlong, but which were not considered worth the effort to reduce, are ruthlessly pruned. However good the original may have seemed, it often appears overlong and rambling in comparison with the clipped version.

Although few enthusiasts would readily agree at first that cutting would be beneficial, it should be tried as an experiment, retaining a copy of the original in case the edited version is unsuccessful. In order to enforce the discipline, imagine that the piece is needed for a broadcast which must be fitted into say three-quarters of the actual running time. Brave souls may use two-thirds or even a half as a basis, although it must be admitted that the latter is a bit drastic, and good material may be lost in the process. Having decided on the running time, stick to it and do not be content until the tape conforms to it.

If, after several playbacks and comparisons with the original, it is genuinely felt that the piece is worse for being without a certain section, then it can be re-inserted. It is not necessary to sort through all the off-cuts in order to identify the required part; it is usually easier to copy it on a short length of tape, from the full-length version, and splice this in. If there is any doubt about any part when cutting it out, it can be kept specially for re-insertion if needed.

It goes without saying that all substandard material should be cut out. It should never have to be necessary to apologise for any part of a recording; if apologetic comments are necessary, the material should have been edited out.

## Erase Editing

Another method of removing unwanted short sections of a recording does not involve cutting and jointing. This is by erasure, which can be effected by running the appropriate section past the erase head with the machine switched to Record. This involves switching on and off part way through the tape, and this could result in clicks appearing on the recording.

There is, too, the risk that the tape will be stopped too late and thereby more than required would be erased. This can be avoided by engaging the Pause button and pulling the marked portion of the tape past the head by hand.

A further difficulty may be introduced by the record head, because the recording bias through the head will give partial erasure, and as the tape in advance of the erase head will be passing the record head too, a few inches of it before the portion to be erased will also be affected. If the material runs close to the unwanted sound, it will be spoiled.

An alternative is to use a permanent magnet. The tape can be marked on the machine, then removed to a flat surface. One of the poles of a small permanent-magnet should be lowered vertically onto the tape at the first marker, then moved smoothly along the tape to the second one, where it is lifted off vertically (see Fig. 6.7). The reason for the vertical approach and removal is to avoid affecting adjacent parts of the recording. The magnet should be kept well away from the tape, and all other tapes except when erasing, as there may be inadvertent erasure of wanted parts of the recording.

Fig. 6.7    Wiping small section of tape with permanent bar magnet. It must be dropped vertically onto the tape and lifted vertically to avoid affecting adjacent areas.

**Fades**

It is also possible to effect a fade-out or fade-in by means of a magnet if this has not been done during recording. The section over which the fade is required is marked, using the tape-speed to determine the length, e.g., a one-second fade will be over a length of $3\frac{3}{4}$ inches at the standard speed. The magnet is lowered onto the tape at the point where the recording ceases, and moved slowly back along the tape, at the same time gradually lifting it from the surface. At the end of the stroke it should be about half-an-inch from the tape, then it is lifted away. Fig. 6.8a shows the magnet path.

It is not easy to control the height of the magnet over the tape so that it follows this path with reasonable accuracy. However, it can be done if the magnet is held between thumb and forefinger with the pole flat on the tape to start. As the stroke proceeds, the thumb, which is resting on the tape, is rolled so that the magnet is gradually lifted off. Fig. 6.8b shows the positions at the start and finish, with one intermediate position. A fade-in can be done in the same way by starting where the recording starts and proceeding along for a predetermined length.

Recordings on any of the other tracks on the tape will also be erased or faded when using a magnet, but these would be ruined anyway if normal editing methods were used. So, any recording which is likely to need editing must be made on a blank tape unless the previous recordings on other tracks are no longer required.

Room ambience, background music or effects are lost by erasure in this manner, but these are also affected by cutting the tape. The magnet method, then, should be confined to cleaning-up pauses between

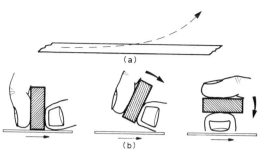

Fig. 6.8  (a) To produce a fade after recording, using a magnet. It must be started in contact with the tape then lifted gradually and evenly away. (b) An even lift can be obtained by rolling the magnet over the thumb slowly as it is passed along the tape.

scenes, or sound-sequence recordings and effects-tapes where there is no recording-room ambience.

Some may raise the objection that a permanent magnet adds noise because it is saturating the tape just as a d.c. erase system in a cheap recorder. However, the effect is slight, and as periods of only a second or two are involved, it is not noticed and in any case it may be masked by the normal recorder noise level. The method should be given a trial to determine whether the noise level is noticeable on the equipment in use.

CHAPTER SEVEN

# RECORDING
# SOUND EFFECTS

MOST TAPE DRAMAS and many other forms of creative tape recording involve the use of sound effects. These can be produced at the time of the recording, but this can be rather inconvenient, especially if they are of a complex nature. It is enough to attend to the various tasks involved in making the recording, without having to supervise the production of realistic sound effects at the same time. Furthermore, some effects may be impossible to improvise with the resources available, and so the completion of the recording may be held up until they can be obtained.

The answer is to have the effects pre-recorded and available at any time they may be required. The creative recordist should set about making a sound effects tape as soon as possible. Effects can be made, or recorded from other sources, whether or not there is any immediate use for them. Thus a collection will be built up and continually added to as opportunity affords. Before long a quite comprehensive library of effects will be available.

The effects should be recorded one after another on the tape, leaving an interval of about ten seconds between each one as a precaution against running on to the next effect when copying-off. The duration of each effect will depend on its nature. Those that are complete in themselves (breaking glass, explosions, etc) will obviously last for as long as they take, in most cases just a few seconds. Continuous sounds such as the sea, rain, thunder storms, crowd noises and traffic sounds require more thought. If too short, they can run out before their time when copying off and mixing in; if too long, they take up unnecessary room on the effects tape, and because of their duration may take longer to locate individually.

About $2\frac{1}{2}$ minutes is a useful duration. This may not sound long, but really it is a considerable time for a sound effect and allows for a safety margin against over-running. Should a longer duration be required, the extra length can be built up by copying the section from the effects tape

94

several times onto a separate tape. This is better than recording direct from the effects tape, stopping, rewinding and restarting at the beginning of the effect. When mastering the final recording, the least complications the better.

## Locating the Effects

Some means of accurately locating required effects with the minimum time spent must be devised. The digital counters fitted to most recorders give only an approximate position and the only reliable method is to mark the tape itself. Chinagraph pencils, which are useful for temporary marking when editing, do not give a lasting inscription, and several times through the recorder past the pressure pads will blur or obliterate any markings.

Special marking tabs for the purpose are available in different colours for colour-coding the contents of a reel. As there can be thirty or more effects to each track on the reel, colour-coding is obviously not the complete answer. Furthermore, the tabs are intended to wrap over the tape from one side to the other in order to be visible from the side of the reel. This increases the width of the tape and creates problems when passing through the tape-guides; also, the double thickness resulting from being on both sides of the tape can displace the pressure-pads. All-in-all, these tabs are not the best way of marking and are not recommended.

## Splicing Tape Markers

One of the most practical methods, and quite a simple one, is to stick about an inch of splicing tape ($\frac{7}{32}$ inch width) on the back of the tape at the start of the effect, in the same way as for making a splice (Fig. 7.1). Being white, it can be inscribed with numbers for indexing, but as the surface is glossy some difficulty may be found in marking it. A black ball-point pen will usually do the trick although the numbers may have to be retraced a few times to make a good clear impression. Frequent running of the tape through the recorder will in time blur and fade the numbers, so that they may need occasional renewing.

Another way of marking the splicing tape is to scratch the number with a sharp point on the sticky side. This will remove the white

Fig. 7.1  Labels consisting of splicing tape inscribed with numerals to indicate the start of a particular effect. The position and underlining of a number readily identifies which track it applies to.

colouring and leave the tape transparent, so that when fixed to the recording tape the number will show up brown. The number must, of course, be inscribed backwards, and the strokes should be made wide so that the number is clearly visible and the surrounding adhesive does not heal over the portion removed.

It may be thought more convenient to place the marker so that it is positioned at some easily-seen spot such as a tape-guide, when the effect starts. Here again, though, we have the problem of what happens when a different recorder is used for playback. It is generally better to put the mark at the actual start on the tape, when it can be set up to start at the playback head. Thus the tape can be used on any instrument. It is not necessary to mark the end of the effect, for if all continuous ones are recorded for the same length (e.g. $2\frac{1}{2}$ minutes), a clock or watch with a second-hand will show how much effect-time is left. This is easier than watching for a finish-marker.

In accord with good recording technique, continuous effects should be faded up at the start and down at the end. This will save fading up at the start when an actual production is being recorded, and should the effect run out just before time, it will sound better than abrupt finish. If a longer duration effect is being made from the effects by repeat copying, the fades will have to be cut out by starting each run just after the fade-up and finishing just before the fade-out.

## Grouping and Indexing

It would make for a tidy arrangement of things if all sound-effects of one kind were grouped together on the tape; e.g. recordings of various types of bells: alarm bells, church-bells, door-bells and chimes, ice-cream van bells etc. The difficulty is that some recordings within each classification would be made at widely differing times, and in the meantime recordings of other sounds would be made and assigned the next consecutive numbers. The tape could, of course, be cut and edited to include later recordings in the same group, but this would throw the consecutive numbering out. One way round this difficulty is to add a lettered suffix to distinguish the individual effects, with the number to describe the group. Thus alarm-bells could be 1a, church-bells 1b, and so on. Later additions would then be assigned the next letter without upsetting the running of the numbers.

Generally, there is no great advantage, but a lot of extra work, in having all the effects of one type all together. Rarely would they be needed on the same occasion. The easiest way is to keep adding each new effect as it is obtained, but to keep the index up-to-date so that similar effects appear under the same heading, with detailed descriptions and the number of the tape where the effect is located.

Fig. 7.2    Many useful sound effects can be obtained from 'life', such as car and train noises.

## Local General Effects

A good many sound effects can be obtained by recording the real thing in and around one's own locality and as most of these will be outdoors a battery portable recorder will be essential. Traffic sounds are easy to obtain by merely standing on the nearest main road and letting the recorder run for a while. Always tape more than the $2\frac{1}{2}$ minutes you intend to use in the final effects-tape, and this applies to all continuous sound effects. There will often be a lull when nothing much seems to be happening and the final result will be an edited version including the most interesting bits. If you do not wish to appear too conspicuous, sit in a parked car with the window down to take the recording!

A car journey can be recorded by simply letting the recorder run while driving round a few blocks. Be sure to include a number of gear changes, even if not strictly necessary for the journey, also a few stops as if at traffic lights and pedestrian crossings. Do not use a car that is too silent in running, otherwise tyre swish and the general roar and rushing of air past the bodywork will obscure the engine noise and the recorded result will not sound particularly like a car ride.

## Particular and Related Effects

Other special traffic sounds that could be recorded include a car door slamming and the car being driven away, a motorcycle starting and moving off. a bus arriving and departing from a bus stop, a heavy lorry starting, also labouring up a hill. This illustrates the point that for any general type of effect such as traffic sounds, there can be many individual items. As the object is to make an effects collection that is as comprehensive and extensive as possible, think when recording a particular effect what related subjects could be also taped.

Another example of a general type of effect covering many particular variations is crowd-noises. These can embrace crowds of many different sizes: a local pub or cafe, a department store, the audience at an interval in a concert or play, a large crowd at a sports meeting. There can be different moods: normal conversation, enthusiastic and boisterous effects, cheering and applause, a hostile crowd. There can also be special crowd noises such as those taken in a swimming bath with its highly reverberant acoustics, or at the seaside on a crowded beach where there is no reverberation, or the unique sound of a crowd of children taken in a school playground.

Many effects will need much patience to record and will therefore be more rewarding when eventually obtained. For example a vigil at the end of the road housing the local fire station on bonfire night may well be rewarded by the sound of a fire engine at full speed with bells and siren going.

### Sources away from Home

A trip into the countryside to the nearest farm could yield a variety of sounds. Cattle, poultry and other farm animals, both separately and together, could be recorded; milk churns clattering, farm equipment such as tractors and harvesters can also be obtained. A visit to the zoo could be a fruitful source of animal sounds of many kinds, but it would be better to choose a quiet time, as wild animal sounds would be more useful without any human accompaniment!

When going on holiday to the seaside, why not take the portable recorder as well as the more usual camera? There are many opportunities here for adding to the collection. There is the sound of the sea on sand or pebble beaches, or dashing against rocks. Then there are beach crowd noises, motor-boats, fairground sounds, seagulls and many others. In each case, try different microphone distances and positions to get the best effect.

### Artificial Methods

Another class of sound effects is those produced by artificial means; ones that would be difficult or impossible to obtain naturally. Strangely enough, some artificial effects sound more realistic than the real thing! This is because it is often difficult to get a suitable microphone

Fig. 7.3    A zoo is a prolific source of animal sounds, but watch the subject and not the level indicator! Automatic control facilities are very useful for this type of recording.

position, or to cut out excessive reverberation or extraneous noise when attempting to record the actual sound. Artificial substitutes can be controlled and experimented with to produce just the required result. Here are some examples of those that can be produced quite easily.

Thunder can be produced by suspending a large sheet of thin metal and shaking it from one corner. Gentle shaking will give the effect of distant rumbles, but a sudden violent start to the shaking followed by gentler ones will sound like a nearby peal followed by its echoes. Another storm sound, that of torrential rain, can be obtained by rolling a quantity of dried peas around in a metal sieve. This could be recorded on its own, and also accompanied by the thunder.

A good impression of waves breaking on a shingle shore can be obtained by putting some dried peas, small pebbles and some gravel in a fibre suitcase, and then rocking it rhythmically back-and-forth. Let the contents slither along the length of the case before pounding at the end, and then wait a fraction of a second before repeating in the opposite direction.

The effect of falling masonry can be obtained in a similar way. Put a small number of small stones in a large cardboard box, then rotate the box slowly, allowing the stones to slide along the inside from corner to corner. The action should not be too regular, with a long slither sometimes and then a short one, to get the most realistic effect. If you have a creaking door in the house, don't oil it—until you have recorded it for a sound-effect! Mixed in with the crashing masonry it sounds like rending timbers, and adds realism. Do not use it more than two or three times during the effect; keep it in the background as it would not naturally predominate over the falling brickwork. It sounds very effective if timed at the beginning of one of the slides of stones in the box.

From this it can be seen that effects using multiple sound sources need to be carefully thought out and planned, and the balance needs controlling just as much as with other recordings. Incidentally, the creak of the door can be recorded on its own as well for its own sake, before being eliminated by the oilcan!

The sound of rustling leaves and undergrowth can be obtained by gently crushing a ball of tissue paper in the hand; if done fairly smoothly with random rises and falls of intensity, the effect will be that of the wind rustling the leaves of trees, but if more vigorously and rhythmically, the effect of footsteps through fallen leaves will be achieved. A sheet of cellophane treated in the same way will give the effect of a roaring fire.

Footfalls on other surfaces can also be successfully imitated. A small cloth bag filled with flour impacted rhythmically will give footfalls in the snow, and a bunch of keys carefully shaken vertically will give the effect of footsteps on gravel, although care must be taken not to allow them to jangle against each other.

Footsteps on pavement are best achieved by recording the real thing, but the effect will be better if shoes with steel tips are worn, and also if the recording is made in a courtyard or narrow street. Sound reflections from the walls of nearby buildings will add to the reverberation and improve the effects. Quite a collection of footstep effects can be made, as in addition to the various surfaces, one can record walking and running steps, single, and several simultaneously, and on the pavement, male and female footsteps. Then of course there can be numerous combinations such as a man and woman's footsteps together running and walking.

**Breaking Glass and China Effects**

A breaking window is quite a useful sound to add to the collection. Dropping pieces of glass does not sound effective because the sound lacks the initial impact. The best way to do this is to support a large piece of unwanted glass several feet over a stone or concrete surface. Then tap the centre with a hammer, not too violently, just sufficiently

Fig. 7.4 The effect of falling masonry being obtained by tipping pebbles and gravel along a long narrow cardboard box.

to break the glass. Thus the sound of the impact and the glass vibrating in mid-air will be followed by the broken glass crashing onto the stonework floor, a quite distinctive and satisfying sound. When recording this effect, a sensible precaution would be to wear leather gloves or gauntlets and a pair of goggles or sun-glasses.

An allied sound is that of breaking crockery but, although similar, it doesn't 'tinkle' like glass, and there is not the intial impact as with a breaking window. A good idea is to save any chipped or cracked china until several pieces have been accumulated. These can then be assembled on a tray and dropped onto a hard (preferably stone) surface. If all the pieces hit the floor at the same time, the effect is short-lived and rather disappointing. A slight delay can be introduced by holding one or two pieces between the fingers and allowing them to fall a fraction of a second later.

The use of coconut shells for hoofbeats is well known, but remember that when used on a padded surface the effect of hoofbeats on grass or earth can be obtained. A foghorn or ship's siren can be imitated by blowing across the top of a bottle; the pitch of the resulting sound can be varied by putting some water in the bottle (the more water, the higher will be the note).

Some good effects can be obtained by recording and playing back at different speeds. A splashing tap recorded at a higher speed will sound like a waterfall or other large volume of water. The effect of a large generator or other piece of heavy machinery can be simulated by recording a vacuum-cleaner at twice the speed of playback. There are almost endless possibilities.

## Radio and Television Sources

A rich source of sound effects is radio and television drama productions. Effects are often heard that would be difficult to obtain naturally or make artificially; a car smash and cattle stampeding have been obtained in this way by the author.

Of course, one does not know in advance what effects are going to be used, so record any likely looking production and then copy off any useful effects. One snag is that dialogue is often superimposed on the effect, but by careful editing sufficient of the effect can be salvaged and lengthened if desired by repeat-copying. Films shown on television are often quite productive in this respect, because there is often a longer gap between dialogue than could be tolerated in a radio play. Unfor-

Fig. 7.5    Sound effects being produced for a production of *Elijah,* a prizewinning entry in the Schools Class of the 1971 British Amateur Tape Recording Contest. *(Photograph by courtesy of Mr. Lloyd-Hughes and the FBTRC).*

tunately, this is frequently filled in with background music, thereby rendering any effects useless!

Recording from radio or TV should be by direct lead from proper output sockets as with copying from another recorder. As quality is not quite so important with sound-effects, use can be made of the extension-speaker sockets if there are no others. With TV sets especially, there is the danger of shock unless the sockets have been fitted by a qualified person and are electrically isolated from the chassis. Do not attempt to do this yourself unless you know what you are doing.

By various means, then, an extensive collection of sound effects can be built up. While such a collection will be a great asset to draw from for future creative productions, it can be considered an end in itself and an example of creative recording, even though some effects have been 'borrowed' from other sources. Some people collect stamps, coins and other objects, and although the individual items are not made by the collector, he is often said to have created the collection.

It is his judgement and skill in acquisition that has brought the various items together, some perhaps of a rare nature, and difficult to obtain. If this is so, how much more is it true of the sound-effects collector whose skill will actually have created many of the items? In itself, collecting sound-effects is an absorbing and creative hobby.

## Copyright Laws

To conclude this chapter, we must say a few words about background music and the copyright laws. The situation is complicated because there are several interests involved. There is the composer's right, the performer's rights and the gramophone companies' rights or those of the broadcasting authority.

The composer's is the simplest, perhaps, because his copyright lapses fifty years after his death, leaving an extensive field of music in the classical category free from copyright problems. However, the performers' interests are looked after by the Performing Rights Society to whom a fee is payable each time the music is played in public, whether the audience have paid for admission or not. Private performances are not affected, but a tape entered for a competition or played at a tape-club would legally attract a fee.

The gramophone companies will permit no copying of a gramophone record whatsoever, even for private purpose (and this would include a small extract for use as a background) unless a dubbing fee is paid. This law is widely broken as is obvious from the large number of record players that have built-in tape sockets, but a tape containing dubbed music from a record which is entered for a competition or broadcast (the BBC sometimes uses amateur-made tapes if of outstanding interest and of high technical quality) could lead to trouble if the fee has not been paid.

Some records are sold specially for dubbing onto tape or film and these provide the easiest way out of the problem. Of course, the repertoire is limited in comparison to that available elsewhere, but there is a fair selection to cover most moods and effects. Some recordists who are musically inclined compose and perform their own music, thereby avoiding copyright problems and taking creative recording to its ultimate!

# CHAPTER EIGHT

# TAPE DRAMAS

---

THE TERM TAPE DRAMA is used to describe any form of play on tape, whether it is serious or comedy. Drama presents many opportunities to exercise creative ability. An existing play can be performed and recorded, or a short-story adapted into a play, or a play can be written especially. The latter is the most creative because you start with nothing except an idea; but the adapted story, and even the existing play, all require modification and this means creative work.

The first thing to remember is that every movement and action must be conveyed aurally, there being no visual component. This may seem obvious, but if you are doing an existing play and the stage directions call for visual effects, how can these be presented? For example, the directions stipulate that the stage is darkened, a window is seen opening and an intruder enters. He is looking for something and opens cupboards and desk-drawers. He moves a couple of pictures on the wall and then finds a wall-safe hidden behind one of them. While attempting to open it, the light suddenly comes on and the householder appears. How can this be conveyed on tape?

## Using a Narrator

One solution is to introduce a narrator to tell the story in between the sections of dialogue. It can be narrated in the third person (as an outside observer) or in the first person, the narrator being one of the characters and taking part in the dialogue as well. A difficulty arises in the relating of events which it is necessary for the audience to know of, but which the character who is the narrator is not supposed to know.

He can do this by inserting a phrase such as '*it was unknown to me at the time, but* . . .' or something similar. If this is done he cannot go into detail in his description as he was not supposed to be there, so a general rather than an eye-witness account would have to be sufficient. Another possibility is to switch to another narrator for the particular sequence, but this rather destroys the continuity.

Using a narrator is an easy way out but with some dramas it could destroy the effect of the action happening as you hear it. It is more subtle to convey what is happening by means of extra or modified dialogue, and by sound effects. This is an art which must be mastered if a narrator is not always to be used. The dialogue must not be forced or unnatural, with one character telling the other what he can see for himself, but the information must be carried by natural comments and ejaculations. The audience must not realize that they are being told what is happening.

## Effects and Dialogue Convey Action

Let us go back to the example. How can we convey that it is dark and at night? A slight wind noise and a distant church clock striking, say, two will give an atmosphere of desolation and emptiness. The complete absence of traffic noises or other sounds of human activity conveys that it is two in the morning and not two in the afternoon. An accomplice can be added in order to provide the dialogue, unless it is essential for the story that the intruder is alone.

The first comment would be for the intruder to tell his companion to shine the torch on the window catch. This confirms the impression of night-time and indicates their intention. Voices would, of course, be in whispers to add further effect. The sounds of an owl hooting could be used as well, but this is rather hackneyed and unnecessary because the time is already well established.

Now for the sound of the window being opened. A sash window should be used here, as this has a characteristic sliding sound, whereas a hinged window is practically silent. Muffled sounds of entry follow, the window is closed and the wind noise immediately ceases—they are now inside. The 'search' is easily indicated by a few words of whispered instruction (*'you look in those cupboards, I'll search the desk'*) then comes the sounds of drawers sliding open and shut and papers rustling. After a pause, *'I wonder what's behind these pictures . . . nothing there . . . ah! as I thought'*, then in a heightened whisper, *'there's a safe over here'*.

This can be followed by a few fumbled remarks about locks and combinations, during which there is a sharp snap of a light switch. There are ejaculations from both men, no longer in whispers, then the householder speaks. Thus the dialogue and sound effects carry the whole action. If it is necessary for the plot that only one character is 'on stage' a similar effect can be obtained by having him speak his thoughts as he performs the various actions, although this sounds rather contrived.

## Special Characters Provide Setting

Sometimes a setting can be described by persons introduced for the purpose and who have no further part in the plot. Let us take a setting that would seem difficult to describe other than by a narrator. Imagine a lighthouse mystery; both keepers have disappeared with trace, all that is left is the unoccupied lighthouse. How could dialogue be used here? First of all, we can have the sound of a ship's engines and the swish of bow-waves.

1ST VOICE: *Hey capt'n, what d'you make of that?*

2ND VOICE: *That's the Point light isn't it?*

1ST VOICE: *Yes but I've never seen its lights on in broad daylight before.*

2ND VOICE: *Here lend me your glasses . . . hm, no sign of life, it is manned isn't it? . . . must be something wrong, get Sparks to send a message to shore . . .*

The setting is thus made and the way prepared for further dialogue as an investigating party is landed at the lighthouse. These two then fade out and do not appear again, having served their purpose. The same thing applies whether recording a stage play, adapting a short story or writing a special play; translate all visual action and settings into dialogue and sound effects.

## Limitations

The tape recordist has not the same limitations as the film-maker when it comes to spectaculars and ambitious presentations. For film there must be sets, suitable locations, costumes and many extras. The recordist's equivalent to these is his sound effects. If he has a sound effect of a chariot race and a roaring crowd at the arena, then he needs only to mix in the voices of his actors and he's *got* a chariot race with his characters in the thick of it. Thus the need for an extensive collection of effects.

The main limitation in a tape drama is the actors themselves. In most cases they will be amateurs, friends and relatives, most of whom will have had no acting experience. This is the weak link; one may have an impeccable technique, have made an excellent job of the play itself and its adaption, and nicely edited it, yet if the actors sound wooden or unnatural, the whole thing is ruined. First of all, then, one must choose or write a play that is within the actors' capabilities, and not attempt anything requiring a degree of acting skill they do not possess. It is better to do a simple piece really well than an ambitious work badly.

In addition to the skill of the actors one must consider their number and availability. There may be three or four persons who are reasonably good, but the script may call for more; to conscript others whose abilities are limited in order to make up the number may be courting disaster. One poor performance could spoil the whole thing. So choose a play for which you can be sure of the required number of actors.

## Voice Quality and Dialect

Voices should not sound too much alike. The audience are not familiar with the characters or even the players; they have to rely on differences of voice to tell them apart. Sometimes, although not often, a radio play is heard where two or more characters have similar-sounding voices, confusing results and obscuring the point of the plot. We should hasten to add that this does not happen very often as the BBC obviously consider this factor when casting parts for their drama productions.

Some voices have unusual characteristics that can be instantly recognised; these are especially useful for tape dramas, but of course they cannot be used for doubling up, i.e. taking more than one part in the same production. Anyone given more than one part should have an 'ordinary' voice that does not stand out, and if possible some attempt at disguise could be tried for one of the parts.

Mechanical aids to voice-disguise have the advantage that they are consistent. These include talking with a boiled sweet in the mouth, lightly pinching the nose, and cupping the hands around the mouth (but not over the mouth as this would muffle the voice and render it unintelligible). Slightly raising or lowering the pitch of the voice may help to produce a good disguise. Vocal disguise, that is one produced purely at the will of the actor, may not be consistent, and he may lapse from time to time into his natural voice.

This brings us to the matter of dialect. The play may call for a regional dialect from one or more of the actors, and unless this is someone that speaks the dialect naturally, it means that it must be assumed. Assumed dialects are always tricky, especially for amateur actors, as they may well be inaccurate or they may drift into another similar dialect, or on occasions into their natural voice. Even if accuracy is maintained, the accent may be more thickly laid on some times than at others. It is wise to avoid using dialect if possible, especially for long or major parts; for small 'bit' parts it may come off if there is someone who can do it well. This factor will also influence one's choice of play.

Choosing an existing play for a tape drama, then, is largely a matter of finding one for which the players are available, and that is within their capabilities to portray. Then it is a matter of adapting it, as we have described, to render it completely aural. Using a short story needs

Fig. 8.1    A recording session for the play *The DDL Programme,* which won first prize in the Schools Class of the 1971 British Amateur Tape Recording Contest. *(Photo courtesy of Mr. Lloyd-Hughes and the FBTRC).*

more adaption, but the general principle is the same. It is the writing of a play from scratch that needs the most work and creative ability. Here we will outline the special requirements of tape dramas and offer some guidance on a few basic points of play-writing for tape.

### Working Out a Plot

One must start with a plot or idea that can be built up into a play. The scope is wide, as almost any setting and field of human relationship can be used. Most plots present the characters with a problem or task, and then describes their attempts to find a solution or fulfil the task. Further problems may arise, or the original one become complicated by such attempts, or by other circumstance. Eventually a solution is reached, either as a result of their efforts, or by some unexpected turn of events (which must of course be probable), or an unexpected result comes from these activities which may be desirable or not so desirable. Thus can be described the majority of story or drama plots.

There can be sub-plots (stories independent of the main one but going on at the same time) but these must have some link with the main plot. One trick is to have the sub-plot apparently unconnected with the main one to start with, but later bringing them together to provide the solution to the main plot or at least to influence the result. An ingenious twist is to not only have the solution of the main plot provided by the sub-plot, but have the solution of the sub-plot brought about by incidents in the main one.

A decision will have to be made as to the nature and treatment of the subject. If it is in serious vein then the rules of probability must be adhered to, but if it is to be a comedy or even a farce, then more improbable happenings can be introduced. Once the treatment has been decided on it must be consistent throughout, and the dialogue treated accordingly. In a serious work, lighter touches can be introduced here and there to relieve the darker tones, perhaps in the sub-plot or by the creation of a faintly comic character in one of the lesser parts.

Get the basic plot down on paper. The three fundamental parts will be problem, attempted solution, and result. Now devise an outline of the progress of the story and its order, which may not necessarily be that of the three basic parts mentioned above. We may start off by finding our main character doing something unusual or exciting, this being the attempted solution to a problem which is not revealed until later. Thus there will be two questions of interest to answer: why is he doing it and what will be the result?

We may even start with the result if it is an unexpected one, and depict what led up to it, the problem and attempted solutions. Usually, though, with such a treatment, there is a final twist which follows the apparent result and which is left to the very end. Otherwise, if all is known in advance, the play is robbed of most of its suspense and interest.

### Interesting Introductions

It is essential that the interest of the audience is captured and held. Nowhere is this more important than at the beginning. There must be an incentive to follow the fortunes and misfortunes of the set of unknown characters, and this should be provided by initial interest and curiosity. The introduction must have impact; something interesting must happen in the first couple of minutes or the audience's attention will wander. A long drawn-out chat between characters about trivial matters at the start will kill interest before the play gets going.

As there is no compulsion to take events strictly in the order they happen, an interesting or exciting sequence can start the play, providing there is a smooth and natural transition into the rest of the story.

Flashbacks can be employed, but these can be overdone so they should be used sparingly if the production is not to seem hackneyed.

There is also a danger of having an arresting opening, riveting the audience's attention, and then allowing the action to flag. This is a common fault with many television films and the result is a feeling of anti-climax. There must be varying heights of tension and interest throughout a drama production, but a 'flat' part coming after a good opening spoils the effect. Try to keep the interest alive at least until the characters become known so that interest in *them* will carry the thing along through the less interesting parts.

Of course an introduction doesn't have to be exciting or action-packed to be interesting. A curious circumstance or unusual incident, or perhaps just a hint of mystery in an otherwise ordinary conversation, can capture the audience.

## Introducing the Characters

Another function of the introduction is to introduce the main characters. The audience wants to know who they are, why they are there, and what they are up to. This should be made clear before the play has run many minutes. We have already seen how action or a setting can be conveyed by carefully worded dialogue. Now, we will take an example to illustrate the introduction of the characters.

A knock is heard at the door. Sounds of typing in the background.

MALE VOICE: *Come in.*

FEMALE VOICE: *Oh Mr. Greenwood, Mr. Rogers rang up while you were engaged on the other line, he asked if you would ring him back. He said it was very urgent.*

MALE VOICE: *Oh he did did he. That'll be a change, in my twenty years with this firm I've yet to see him treat anything as urgent. Oh, by the way Miss Smith, would you take these papers over the managing director's office straight away, Mr. Carson wants them without delay.*

Now let us analyse this dialogue. We have established that Mr. Greenwood holds some executive position in a firm for which he has worked for twenty years and has his own office and secretary named Miss Smith. The managing director is named Mr. Carson, and he has an office nearby. Mr. Rogers has an as yet unspecified status, but he is not particularly energetic, and he wants to speak to Greenwood urgently. The interest is provided by that note of urgency. The audience will be wondering why it is urgent; there must be something unusual for him to behave out of character. Notice that it takes longer to actually state these points than to bring them out in carefully worded dialogue.

## Writing Dialogue

Dialogue is for many a difficult thing to write, and the result often sounds unnatural and stilted. We must certainly learn to master this art, as our whole production is made up of it. Think of your character, not as just a player in the drama, but as a real-life person. Think of his status in the firm, community or social group among whom the action of the play takes place. Think of his background, his attitudes to work, society, and his family. Think of the sort of education he has had. Make a note of this picture with these details, along with his physical characteristics such as age, height, build, colouring, etc.

Many of these points will never be revealed in the play because it will be unnecessary, but they will provide a clear picture of the character. Whenever you are writing lines for him, ask yourself how would he react in the situation you are creating for him? What would he say? How would he say it? Imagine him saying those things, imagine yourself in his place and say the lines out loud. Do they seem natural for him, or are they not quite right?

It can be appreciated that there is more to writing dialogue than just putting words into character's mouths. However, if the character behaves always as expected, then we say that he is flat, like a cardboard cut-out, he is not 'in the round'. This is because people are a mixture of different emotions and characteristics; one sort may be predominant, but others come to the surface at times, especially when under stress or faced with unusual circumstances. So, let your characters sometimes behave 'out of character' and they will become real.

## The Conclusion

Work through your plot, introducing and building up your characters as well as the story until you come to the finale. Here, the threads of the story are tied up, the solution or end-result presented, and we take our leave of the characters. The final lines wind up the whole thing nicely and should leave the audience feeling that a satisfactory conclusion has been reached. There is, however, a modern trend to abolish such an end. The argument goes that life doesn't present its solutions in neat parcels, it just goes on, often with an unsatisfactory result. So many modern plays finish without a conventional conclusion. Some for that matter do not have a conventional plot; they are just a slice of life with no beginning, no story and no end.

Whether such a production is satisfying for the players is questionable; it rarely is for the audience, who usually feel cheated and disappointed. The whole object is to tell a story, a complete plot, and when no real story emerges, the result is colourless and empty, even though it may be more like life. Some playwrights and authors, like workers in other forms of art, try to be different at any cost and to

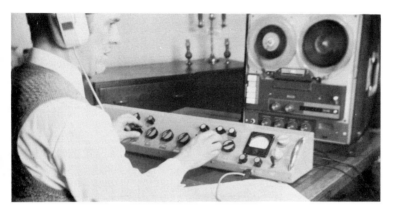

Fig. 8.2    Taping a drama. The mixer, designed, built and operated by the author, has seven microphone inputs, gram and tape inputs, a.g.c., meter level indicator, tone controls and monitoring facilities.

thereby gain notoriety and fame. Often they defeat their own ends because so many others are trying to do the same, and so modern drama (like some modern art and music) has become gimmicky and hackneyed. Such works are often praised by those who feel they will be considered old-fashioned and out-of-touch if they do otherwise, and so the whole thing tends to be self-perpetuating. It sometimes seems that the really original writer today is one who produces a really good plot with a well-rounded-out finish!

### Casting

Having written the play or made the adaptation, the time comes to start preparing for the recording. Casting is the first consideration. If a play has been selected or written to suit a certain group of players, the casting will be automatic. If one is fortunate to have a wide circle of acquaintances who could take part then a selection has to be made of those who appear to be most suitable for the parts.

It is good to choose individuals who are most like the characters in the play; well-spoken persons for those characters who are well-educated or who have a high status or position, more 'earthy' types for those in humbler positions, a talkative person for a character who is likewise, and so on. Thus by being themselves, at least as regards speech, a good portrayal of the character will be assured. Look out, too, for those with an unusual voice quality, as mentioned before.

**The Script**

Next, copies of the scripts must be typed, double-spaced and with wide margins to allow for alterations made during rehearsals. Scripts typed on thin paper rustle when turned and if several copies are turned at the same time the noise will appear on the recording. Thick paper, such as cartridge-paper, could be used but as carbon copies cannot be made each copy must be written individually. Alternatively, carbon copies can be made and secured to thick paper by a dab of paste in each corner. Later, they can be torn off and the thick sheets used again. Use one side only so that the sheets do not have to be turned over; the actor can remove the top one when it is finished and put it on the bottom. The stiffness will enable him to hold the script in one hand and leave the other free.

Get the actors to take their scripts home and learn as much as possible. This may not seem to be necessary as they will have the script before them when recording. However, if they are thoroughly familiar with their lines, they will speak them fluently and naturally, and it will not sound as if they are being read out.

**Rehearsals**

Several rehearsals will be needed. At the first one, note if the dialogue flows naturally and smoothly and if all sections sound right. If not, try to analyse what is wrong. Ask the actor if he feels that the lines are what the character would say. Having studied the part and learned much of it, he may be able to offer constructive suggestions. Do not be afraid to adapt and modify even at this late stage.

Having been satisfied that the play is satisfactory, rehearsals should concentrate on the way the players say their lines, the pauses and so on. If you have quite definite ideas as to how a line should be delivered, show the actor how you want it, get him to repeat it after you. On the other hand, give the players some freedom to interpret the part as they feel, remembering that you chose them because they resemble the character they are portraying to some extent. They may well add something to the part that you did not envisage; always be open to suggestions on any point.

Do not over-rehearse. This is a rule followed by many professional stage directors. Actors seem to improve to a point when they reach a peak, and then decline. Afterwards, there is often a loss of freshness and spontaneity. So, the professionals often rehearse to the point where it seems that just a little more polish and rehearsal is needed, and then leave it there. The next time through will probably be the best one.

Of course, it is not necessary to do the play right through at one go; it could be rehearsed and recorded one scene at a time. It may be less taxing to the players to have only one scene to concentrate on, and there is a good psychological effect of knowing that there are a number of successful scenes safely 'in the can'.

## Dealing with Mistakes

If a player muffs a line, do not start all over again. This can be discouraging, and, if it happens several times, as is quite likely, it is frustrating to the players who have made no mistakes to have to go over everything again. They may have given a very good performance up to then, and may be irritated that all this has been wasted. Also everyone will be going beyond the peak, quality is likely to fall off and the possibility of more mistakes will increase.

Instead, take them back to some point a few lines before the mistake, and proceed from there. Do not run the recorder back to find the place (which will produce a click on the tape when switching back to Record) but press the Pause button until they are ready to start again, and carry on. The mistake can be edited out afterwards. In any case, there is usually some tension after a mistake and going back to find the place in order to erase the mistake will likely add to it.

It is a good idea to record each scene two or three times, then later select the best one. This is psychologically beneficial to the players, because with several takes being taped they will be less concerned to avoid mistakes, and consequently less self-conscious. It may be noted here that a slight hesitancy here and there, or one or two 'ums' and 'ers', can sound more natural. So a word-perfect performance may not necessarily be the best one.

## Appropriate Acoustics

Microphone technique was covered in a previous chapter, but ensure that the acoustics match the material to be recorded. For example, if characters are on a beach in the open air and then enter a cave, there must be a corresponding change of reverberation. It may mean moving the microphones away from the actors to increase reverberation while turning up the recording level to maintain the same volume level, or it may mean stopping in the middle of the scene and transfering operations to a reverberant room.

## Adding Sound Effects

Effects can be added at the time of the recording by playing them on another recorder and mixing. This is quite suitable for continuous-noise effects, but regular or rhythmic ones may be disrupted by later editing, so it is best to add these when the editing is completed. But there can be complications.

Consider a scene where the action takes place amid raging seas or a howling gale. Whether added later or at the time by being mixed in, the actors will not hear the effects and will be speaking their lines in a perfectly quiet room. To give a realistic performance, it would be necessary to half-shout the lines over the sounds of the elements, not easy to keep up in perfect silence!

Under these circumstances it would be better to play the sound effects so that they can be heard in the recording room and have the volume up so that the actors will really have to shout their lines to be heard. It would not normally be necessary to mix-in as the microphone will pick up the sound. However, if the recorder used to play the effects doesn't sound too well because of having a small loudspeaker or a small plastics cabinet, then a direct-wire feed can be arranged as well, to be mixed-in in the normal way. The recorder can be placed behind the microphones so that the actors can hear it, but there will be little pickup by the microphones.

In most cases, there will be no need to mix by direct wire, and the microphones can be allowed to pick up from the loudspeaker of the effects recorder. This will need some experiment to get the right position so that the effects are heard but do not drown out the actors.

A general point on sound effects is to not overdo them or allow them to become dominant. There is a temptation, having spent much time, effort and ingenuity in creating a particularly good effect, to give it the centre of the stage. One must remember that it is only an effect to add to the realism of the story. If the story is slowed up by too many and too lengthy effects, or if the level is too high so that it becomes difficult to hear the dialogue, then the effects detract from rather than add to the story.

# CHAPTER NINE

# INTERVIEWS

---

IT MAY BE THOUGHT that conducting an interview is hardly an example of creative recording, especially when judged by the standards of the appalling boring examples heard on radio and television. However, if the interview is well handled and creatively edited, the result can be an absorbing, often amusing, record which in time could even become of historical value. It is not fiction, but real people talking about actual events and experiences.

Nearly all interviews are conducted on the interviewee's home ground, so a battery portable is essential for this type of recording. It may not be possible always to have strict control of the recording level, so an automatic model would be very useful.

### Selecting the Subject

Suitable subjects include people who have offbeat occupations, have had a lifetime rich with unusual experiences, or have undertaken some difficult or unusual task or journey. This is one reason why the TV interviews are so uninteresting; they feature people who just happen to be in the news, and they and their opinions are often of little interest to those not directly concerned. Many are politicians or show business personalities who are used to the limelight and have stock answers ready for the interviewers' questions.

Some of the most interesting interviewees are people who are unknown to the world at large. Part of the pleasure and skill in obtaining interviews comes from finding the subjects in the first place. Older or retired persons would be the most likely candidates, especially those with interesting jobs, e.g. the old seafarer who now runs trips around the bay may have spent an earlier period of his life on ocean-going craft and have a wealth of fascinating stories to tell. A police officer may have memories of baffling cases, unusual ones, or ones that were solved by ingenious means. A retired prison warder perhaps could tell of dealings with notorious criminals and some facts and incidents that never became public knowledge.

Coastguards, customs officers, retired engine-drivers may all have exciting stories to tell. Even more common place occupations that entail travel and meeting the public, such as taxi drivers, AA patrols and the district nurse may involve surprisingly interesting experiences. In these days of mass-production, true craftsmen are few, and usually are in older and dying professions. Often these are to be found in cottage industries or one-man firms. The discovery of one of these could well lead to a rewarding interview. If in time the craft eventually died out, your recording could be a valuable link with the past and preserve information that otherwise would have been lost.

It perhaps can now be seen what fascinating possibilities there are and the above suggestions are only some examples of the type of individual who could be the subject of a good interview. Some of the subjects may have a strong regional accent and this will add a welcome flavour and interest to the recording.

### Putting the Subject at Ease

Many people 'dry up' when faced with a microphone, or at least become ill at ease. Some older folk may be even suspicious and doubt the motives of the interviewer. These are problems which must be overcome by one way or another. Matters will almost certainly be made worse by thrusting a microphone into the face of the unfortunate victim when recording commences. Handle it as unobtrusively as possible, keeping it low, out of the direct line of vision, so that once the subject warms up to his story, he will forget all about it.

Even the size of the microphone could have a psychological effect on the subject; a large ball-end with a massive wind-shield is likely to have a very intimidating effect. A small pencil-type would be much better. If the microphone has an on/off switch to control the recorder, the recorder can be placed out of sight or kept slung over the shoulder by a strap if it is of that type.

Some recorders can be run without the subject knowing it. The instrument is operated in a shoulder carrying-case, and the pencil microphone can be clipped like a pen in the top breast pocket. A separate on/off switch can be operated from another pocket. Some may feel that this is unethical, akin to 'bugging' telephones and the like. However, it is not private conversation that is being recorded, the subject is not discussing anything of a secret or confidential matter, otherwise he would not be talking about such things to a stranger. If it is thought that the idea of being recorded would inhibit the subject there can be little harm in recording the conversation without his

Fig. 9.1    A keeper at the Bristol Zoo recalls some of his experiences during a tape interview.

knowing. If one does have any qualms on the matter, the subject can be told afterwards that he had been recorded and the offer made to erase it if he has any objection.

## The Preliminary Encounter

How can an individual be approached with a view to obtaining an interview? First of all, a casual conversation must be struck up to discover whether in fact a worthwhile interview will result. The prospective subject may have little to relate or be inarticulate. Ask a few general questions to assess the prospects and to see in what direction the most fruitful line of enquiry would be during a recorded interview.

For example the old seafarer could be asked 'I expect you've sailed in rougher waters than these?' This could be followed by questions as to places visited, what they were like, what type of ships he sailed in, how old he was when he went to sea, the closest he'd been to a shipwreck, if he had had any strange experiences at sea, and others which may suggest themselves as the conversation continues. These should not be asked in a cold perfunctory manner, but conversationally and showing real interest in the replies; suitable interjections of surprise and wonderment can be made at the right places. You can then say you were so interested that you wonder if he'd mind telling some of it again and letting you record it. In most cases the subject will be flattered by this and will readily agree.

E

Arrange to meet somewhere quiet (a corner of the local pub in an offpeak time will usually be acceptable, and carry for the subject the prospect of free drinks!). In the meantime marshal some of the things you want to come out in the interview, and the order you want them to appear. You can then ask direct questions about specific incidents and thus control the way things go.

## Drawing the Subject Out

Never state facts yourself, merely draw out the subject with your questions. If you want to start at the beginning of his career, ask for example '*You were telling me that you ran away to sea as a lad. Would you like to say just how this happened and how old you were?*' Do not say, '*Is it true that you ran away from school when you were thirteen and joined the s.s. Adventurer as a cabin boy?*' because the only answer to this is 'yes', and you won't finish up with a particularly exciting interview!

You may get him to expand on some of the things that he told you before, or explore any new avenue which seems promising. As the interview gets near to its end you must devise a conclusion. Do not just finish and leave the whole thing up in the air, moreover get your subject to have the last word. This can easily be done by a question such as '*Can you say then that you have had an exciting life at sea?*' or '*Are you glad you ran away to sea as a boy?*' If one question fails to produce an answer with the note of finality try something else, because you must have this to satisfactorily conclude the recording.

## What Kind of Information

The information you seek will usually be of a non-technical nature; human interest and experiences that anyone can listen to and enjoy. Thus, in interviewing an AA patrolman, you would not ask about the types of faults that he had been called to (unless you had a specialised interest as a do-it-yourself car-owner) but about the people he had met, ways in which he had been able to assist other than technical car breakdowns, reaction of road users to various situations, and the usual experiences. Always ask interviewees if they have had any strange or unexplained experiences in the course of their lives or professions. It is surprising the number of strange things that happen to ordinary folk in the course of their lives and never get reported.

One exception to the rule about technical questions would be when interviewing a craftsman, say, for example, a roof-thatcher. Any information about materials, how the work is carried out or the tricks of the trade would be of interest, because of its unusual nature. It could

Fig. 9.2 When taping interviews out of doors it is often useful to use a windshield over the microphone, as shown on this Beyer model M101 omnidirectional dynamic unit.

well prove a unique record of the craft if it eventually died out. Of course, craftsmen are not usually anxious to part with their trade secrets, but a little cajoling may elicit a few points that could prove of value.

## Cutting Out the Questions

Having got the interview on tape, it must be edited. The main job is to cut out all questions and other comments of the interviewer. The result will no longer sound like an interview, but will play back as a subject relating the various incidents and details in the form of a talk, this being far better than having the interviewer's voice intruding at various points and distracting attention from the subject and his story.

This provides another reason why the interviewer must not state facts and get the subject to agree, but must draw them out from him so that when the interviewer's prompting is removed, the subject appears to be recalling things naturally from his memory. This explains, too, why some concluding statement must be elicited from the subject, because the interviewer will not be able to round things off in his own words.

Rather more is involved in this operation than just cutting out the interviewer's voice. There will undoubtedly be many references by the

E*

subject to the interviewer's questions, some may even repeat parts of the question. All these allusions will have to be edited out, and this is where skill and creativeness play their part. Chopping out a sentence or a phrase must leave the remainder making sense and not sounding as though there had been a cut. Voice inflections play their part in this; an injudicious cut may bring together a passage where the subject was speaking slowly and quietly, in a reflective mood, with one where he was more animated, and the change would be very noticeable. It may be necessary to cut out more in order to achieve a smooth join.

### Further Editing

Other things that will need editing out include overlong pauses, hesitation, false-starts, corrections and interruptions. However, do not carry this polishing up process too far; a certain hesitation or minor mistake here and there will add to the effect of spontaneity and naturalness, and will enhance the result. Although the order of the material will have been planned and controlled by the order of the questions, second thoughts may be entertained on hearing the tape, so re-arrangement of the material can be included in the editing process if desired. It can be seen that there is much more involved in the editing of interviews than with most other forms of creative tape recording.

The success of the result depends to a great extent on the skill shown here. Many of the talks broadcast on BBC radio are in fact edited interviews and in most cases are excellent examples of the art. These are equally as good illustrations of how it *should* be done, as the TV news interviews are of how it should *not*. Of course, radio broadcasts allow time for careful planning and editing, which the TV news interviews do not, and the latter also have the handicap of vision editing.

The most straightforward way of editing is to do it as you go. Unlike the tape drama there is no detailed script to study beforehand to enable cuts to be planned in advance. Just load up the tape onto a recorder and start playing. Listen to how the subject responds to your first question, and determine just where you will start. Cut out all before this, join up your leader tape and proceed. Every time you come to a question, interruption, or anything else that needs cutting out, listen carefully to what follows, and decide just where you will pick up the narrative again. Cut accordingly, splice, and continue. Finally play the whole thing through uninterrupted, to get the overall effect, and note any further trimming or alterations that may be required.

# CHAPTER TEN

# SOUND SEQUENCES

WE HAVE ALREADY SEEN that one aim of the creative tape recordist is to build up a comprehensive collection of sound effects. This can be an absorbing hobby in itself, and provides invaluable material to draw on for tape dramas. A further use is in the composition of sound-sequence tapes, collections of sounds strung together to form a particular sequence. They afford considerable scope for creativeness and originality, and generally are easy to produce. There are no actors to direct, interviewees to prompt, nor, in fact, is there any microphone work at all. There is just dubbing off the required sounds, and occasionally mixing, although sometimes live microphone recordings may also be involved.

## Sound-Story Sequence

There are many forms a sound-sequence tape can take. It is possible, for example, to tell a complete story by means of sounds alone, with no spoken words by actors or narrator. Consider the following sequence: First, street sounds for a few seconds, then the sound of breaking glass followed by an alarm bell. Next sounds of running feet, a car door being opened and slammed, then the car driven off at high speed. Another car is heard with a siren, the two cars are heard alternately with brakes squealing and tyres screeching. Then, after the first car is heard to pass, there is a clanking of level-crossing gates and the second car slows and stops, its siren dying down. A train passes slowly, goods trucks clanking along the line, and as it dies away into the distance, the gates open and the car is driven away, the siren picking up again.

Now we hear the first car slow down and stop, hurried footsteps and car doors being slammed, then another car starts up and is driven away at speed. After a fade out and a second or two pause this car is heard to slow down and turn down a gravel path, the gravel under the tyres making its unmistakable sound. A few more seconds later and it stops.

In the distance the car with the siren is heard approaching at speed, but it dies away again as it passes the end of the path.

Footsteps on gravel follow, there is the sound of creaking hinges and doors scraping the ground, the car starts and is driven forward to stop again. Now comes the sound of a struggle with blows falling, scuffling and objects being overturned. Footsteps are heard running away over the gravel, to be followed by others. Then they are heard clambering over rocks and shingle with the sound of the sea coming in from the distance, but getting gradually closer.

## Making the Action Clear

The end of this 'story' can be left to the reader to devise, but the sequence serves to illustrate the sound story. Care must be taken to make the action perfectly clear by the nature of the sounds and how they are brought in. For example, there are three cars involved in the above sequence, so something must be done to identify them. The car with the siren is obvious, but how can the first getaway car be differentiated from the second one? The answer is by recording cars with widely different sounding engines, e.g. a normal saloon, a sports car, etc.

Notice, too, how the action of the car turning off the road is obtained by using a gravel path; without sight or speech, this would be impossible to convey without using a radically different-sounding road surface. Every stage and every action must be carefully thought out to render it understandable without the aid of words. Thus it requires an even greater degree of ingenuity than the tape drama, where the dialogue can be used to convey much of the action.

So, while it is simpler in the actual making, it is more difficult in the invention. It constitutes a real challenge to the script-writer and the resources of his recorded-sounds library, although many of the sounds needed will probably have to be specially recorded, but they can then be added to the library to swell the collection.

A commonly held opinion is that a radio play or tape drama is more gripping to the listener than a film or television play, because he has to visualise the scenes for himself, and so is made to participate. With the sound-story, participation is taken a state further; the listener has no voices to indicate the nature of appearance of the characters and so must use his imagination to an even greater degree.

A variation to the sound-story is to introduce just a few lines of dialogue at the end, to give a twist to the story. Thus, in our opening example, the story could end by a few words spoken by one of the robbers after disposing of the rebellious accomplice, revealing that she was a woman. Or a sequence which is made purposely ambiguous can be cleared up in the end by a few spoken words, perhaps in an unexpected way. For example, a sinister-sounding sequence could be revealed in the end to be just children at play.

The use of pauses and fades to indicate changes of location and time needs to be carefully judged because there can be no confirmation of such changes by means of dialogue as in the case of the tape drama. If the listener misses the change there is nothing to back it up and confusion will result.

## Impressionist Sequence

Another, perhaps more subtle, arrangement of sounds is the impressionist sequence. A good example is an impression of a summer day. There are many sounds that suggest the different aspects of this subject; the continuous roar of traffic on a holiday route to the coast, the hubbub of a crowded beach and children shouting at play, with the frequent outcome of a display of tears! A contrast could be a quiet, peaceful meadow in the countryside, which could be conveyed by the intermittent buzzing of a bee or other insect, distant lowing of cattle or sheep, and perhaps the sound of a harvester in the distance. A fitful breeze rustling leaves in the trees, and maybe the sound of a brook or stream, are also suggestive of summer in the country. Even the

Fig. 10.1   At the Agricultural Show. Recording one of the sections of a natural sound sequence—at the cider tasting booth!

impression of a clear cloudless blue sky can be achieved by the sound of a small single-engined aircraft flying high, something not usually heard in dull cloudy weather, because if such flights are made the sound does not penetrate the cloud for long.

The creativity here is demonstrated not only by choice of subject and recording skill, but by the actual sequence, one sound following logically from the other like the beach scene following the traffic noises, and the juxtapositioning of various subjects, like the contrast between the noise and bustle of the popular resort with the quiet and peace of the countryside.

Many other sounds could be added to show the many facets of a summer day. A game of beach cricket could be heard, with location suggested by the distant sound of the sea, cutting suddenly to a game on the village green with the distinctive sound of leather on willow and mild applause from the crowd. A natural follow up could be the teams reviving their energies in the local pub after the match!

## Linking the Sounds

It must be remembered that a *sequence* is needed, not just a random collection of sounds. There must be something to link them together other than the broad outline of the subject, each sound preparing for and leading into the next. An introduction and conclusion should be

Fig. 10.2　Recording another section at the cattle pens in the natural sounds sequence at the Agricultural Show.

devised to start and round off the recording. In this case a spectacular start would be the dawn chorus of birds—but you would have to get up early to record it! Alternatively, the village clock striking seven, followed immediately by the traffic roar, would indicate that the day trippers are off early on their jaunt. A conclusion could be made of the landlord calling time in the local pub and the regulars leaving.

There are many possible impressionist sequences; take the sea. The sounds of bathers in the surf and motorboats could convey its use for pleasure, then the sound of a liner weighing anchor, with siren going, and the propellers swishing as the liner leaves port, suggests the sea as a means of travel. Recordings of trawlers unloading, with the screaming of gulls and a quayside fish auction, portray its harvest. Rough seas with waves crashing onto the rocks and the sound of distress rockets streaking skyward, the noise of a lifeboat maroon and subsequent launching, can give the other side of the coin.

## Natural Succession Sequence

A further type of sound sequence is that of the natural succession, such as a trip up the river in a rowing boat. The sequence would be of various sounds in the order they occur; a wharf with barges or other vessels of transport being loaded or unloaded, the chatter and sound of crockery or glasses from riverside tea gardens or pubs, wildlife such as geese or ducks, other river craft, and so on. Throughout would be the rhythmic creak and splash of the oars and rowlocks. A shower of rain could be included, accompanied by a quickening of the rowing! Distance would be suggested between some of the sounds by fading out the oar sounds and then fading back in, possibly a little slower, to show that the rower is tiring.

Another example of this genre could be a stroll along the front at one's favourite seaside resort, sounds recorded including a Punch and Judy show, amusement park, customers being served at a sea-food stall, beach games, a barker advertising boat trips, and others. The link would be the footsteps of the stroller, slowing and sometimes stopping at points of particular interest, and quickening past those that were not. This will convey the personality of the recordist, indicating his own taste and preferences. The stroll could continue along to the quieter part to be found in most resorts and end with a few minutes of just the sound of the sea against the rocks and the gulls. Thus a contrast is afforded between the sounds of human activity and those of nature.

As the sequence is ready made, this type of recording may sound deceptively simple, but there is more to it than just letting the recorder run; it must be planned first. A sequence might seem interesting but when recorded lack much of audible interest; it may not be always possible to tell just what is happening from the sounds, because they are not sufficiently informative. So in the planning state it must be determined what is required in each case to convey the complete picture.

When the particular sound source is reached, however, it may be found that things are not as planned. For example in the seafront stroll, the sea-food stall may have no customers when you arrive, the Punch and Judy show may have finished, and the boat-trip barker gone to tea. It may, therefore, be necessary to record some items on another occasion, or perhaps to make two or three recordings at different times, and select the one that most closely approaches that which was planned.

There will be long periods between some features when nothing much of audible interest happens, and these will need to be cut. However, do not cut them out completely, as it will then sound as though everything was crowded together. During such intervals there will be background sounds which will lend atmosphere and presence, so a certain amount should be retained. Synchronising the connecting sounds, such as oars or footsteps in our two examples, when editing will have to be carefully done to avoid making cuts and joins obvious.

## The Abstract Sequence

In the abstract sound-sequence there is no story or theme to tie all the sounds together, but each sound is connected to its successor by an abstract link. The process is similar to uncontrolled thought, in which various notions spring into the mind, apparently without reason but usually with some connection that prompted it from the previous one. Alternatively it could be compared to the party game where two objects are given and one has to establish a series of links via a stated number of intermediates. This is a very personalised art-form.

The links can be a relationship of type, kind or natural association, similar sounds, personal or purely abstract. Let us consider an example. To start, we hear the sound of tea things clattering, followed by a natural association, a whistling kettle. Next, the whistle of a steam train, the connection being a similar sound and steam, followed by the roar and clicking of passing coaches over the rails. Then, the sounds of a busy railway station, echoing footsteps and the noise of porters' trucks, with the station p.a. system coming on with train announcements.

Here there is a quick cut to the p.a. announcing contestants at a sports meeting, a similar-type link followed by audience cheering and applauding. Sustained and steady applause follows (as heard at the end of a prom concert) and here we have a break in the direct or natural links, because the next sound is that of heavy rain. The link is purely of similarity because the two sound very much alike. A natural result follows, the sound of flood waters flowing with the rain continuing. Next, another flow of water, with river sounds and the rowing boat.

The sequence could be extended almost indefinitely, but it serves to illustrate the sort of links that can be made. As to an introduction and conclusion, no hard and fast rules can be made because the whole thing is of an abstract nature. However, a start with ordinary everyday sounds such as the whistling kettle, helps to tie the things down to reality. Flights of fancy and excursions into more exotic realms can then follow. It is like someone day-dreaming whose thoughts are sparked off by some commonplace event or happening.

The conclusion will depend on the way the sequence is going and the nature of the final effects. A neat end is to bring it full circle back to the beginning, starting and finishing with the same effect. Thus, in the example, the rowing boat could give way to a cargo boat being brought into dock by tugs, then sounds of unloading of casks and chests with perhaps a line or two of dialogue from 'dockers' to indicate that the cargo is tea, and finally the crockery and whistling kettle as the beginning. Such a conclusion could, of course, easily become hackneyed.

## Connecting and Mixing

The manner in which the sounds follow each other on the tape can be made to vary according to the effect that it is desired to create. We can cut directly from one to the other without any gap in between, which would be quite effective going from the kettle to the train whistle in the example. There can be pauses of various lengths, and also fades as with other types of work. A further method is to merge the two together, fading in one before the other is finished and then fading out the first. This is useful where very similar sounds follow each other, such as the applause and the rain, and emphasises the similarity.

It may be necessary to mix two or more sounds together in any of these sequences, and this could raise a problem if both were recorded on different parts of the same sound-effects tape. Three recorders can be used to do the mixing, and the portable battery instrument can be used with the main and secondary recorder. One of the required effects can be dubbed off onto the portable, the other played on the secondary recorder with the first effect being played on the portable, and both are then fed into the main recorder for mixing and recording. Merging of sounds as noted above can be carried out in this way.

If three sounds are needed together, the tape of the two can be removed from the main recorder and played on the secondary one, while the third effect (having been dubbed onto the portable) is now played back on it, and so the three effects are fed into the main one for final recording. An alternative arrangement is to use a 4-track recorder with parallel replay as machine A; this requires the use of only two machines.

## Musique Concrete

It may be thought that this would be more appropriately dealt with in the next chapter, which is on music, but although the term 'music' appears in the designation and it is regarded as such by its advocates, it is really nothing like music in its accepted form but is much closer to one of our sound sequences. It consists of sounds, some made by musical instruments (but not necessarily, in fact the majority are not) which are strung together to form a sequence. The main feature is that the sounds are altered literally beyond all recognition.

Thus, the sequence is devised not to provide a link between the sounds, but to produce interesting effects by the way the sounds are doctored and by the order in which they are assembled. It is purely sound for the sake of it with little meaning behind it. The term *musique concrete* signifies that the sounds are from concrete or actual sources

Fig. 10.3   Musical effects, and even a simple tune, can be produced by glasses partly filled with water, for musique concrete effects.

obtained via a microphone, as opposed to 'electronic music' where the sounds are not sounds at all to start with but electrical waves generated by special equipment and recorded directly into the tape.

Many become prejudiced against musique concrete because they come to expect the usual associations of music (harmony, melody and counterpoint) and when none of these are to be heard, only a succession of unrecognisable noises, they turn against it with understandable scorn. Forget the term 'music'; regard it as an interesting sequence of unusual sounds, some beautiful, some grotesque. To compare it with conventional music is really rather pointless.

Some of the equipment needed to modify the sounds would be out of the reach of the amateur home tape-recordist; however, for those wishing to experiment in this field there is much that can be done without expensive apparatus.

## Altering Speed and Pitch

Sounds take on a completely different character when heard at a different speed because this also alters the pitch. With a 3-speed machine it is possible to obtain playback at twice or four times faster or slower, according to the recording and playback speed combinations selected. A problem arises, however, with intermediate speeds as it may be required to obtain a whole range of different speeds to achieve a particular effect, even to use the sound at its different speed-pitches to make a simple tune. The answer is to effectively increase the diameter of the drive spindle to increase the speed.

Many battery portables are supplied with a detachable sleeve that slips over the spindle and is secured by a thumbscrew which is screwed down through the top of the spindle. This is double the circumference of the spindle, hence will drive the tape at twice the speed. If the recordist wishes to take up musique concrete seriously, he will find a set of such sleeves very useful, and if he can get work done on a precision lathe, they could be turned out quite easily.

To be able to reproduce a complete octave of the musical scale with its semitones, twelve sleeves will be required. Accurately measure the diameter of the drive spindle by means of a micrometer to obtain the inside diameter of the sleeves; outside diameters can then be calculated from the Table 10.1, the right-hand column showing the factor by which the spindle diameter must be multiplied.

A practical difficulty will arise with the smaller sleeves because the inside and outside diameters will be so close as to make the sleeve walls impractically thin. The answer is to make the outside diameter twice the size, then play it at half the speed or dub it at double speed. The first four would need to be made in this way, but as the sleeve size depends on spindle size, it may be necessary to make more at double size if the recorder spindle is very thin. In theory, all sleeves could be made this way, eliminating the need to keep changing speeds, but in practice the larger ones would be nearly four times the original spindle diameter and may not clear the pinch-wheel in the off position. All should be labelled in some way to distinguish them, as the minute differences would make it difficult to do so by sight.

If the sleeves are made for a portable machine with sleeve speed-change facilities there will be no problem in securing each sleeve with the thumbscrew. If made for a mains machine, some means of fixing them to the spindle must be devised. It would not be easy to drill down through the top of the spindle and tap out a thread for a thumbscrew, and in any case there would have to be a lower ledge on the spindle to support the bottom of the sleeve. The easiest way, other than making the inside diameter a press fit over the spindle, is to cut two horizontal slots, one on each side of the sleeve through the walls, and secure it with a steel-wire finger-clip as shown in Fig. 10.4c.

## Simple Speed Changes

If speed changes are desired without accurate pitch determination, the easiest way is to use a battery recorder and merely slow it down by touching the paying-out spool with the hand, the degree being controlled by the amount of pressure used. The grip of the pinch-wheel

| Pitch | Multiplying Factor | Double Value for Small Sized Sleeves | Pitch | Multiplying Factor |
|-------|--------------------|--------------------------------------|-------|--------------------|
| A  | 1·0   | —     | E  | 1·5   |
| B♭ | 1·062 | 2·124 | F  | 1·586 |
| B  | 1·124 | 2·248 | F# | 1·684 |
| C  | 1·188 | 2·376 | G  | 1·782 |
| C# | 1·261 | 2·522 | G# | 1·890 |
| D  | 1·333 | 2·667 | A  | 2·0   |
| E♭ | 1·416 |       |    |       |

**Table 10.1**

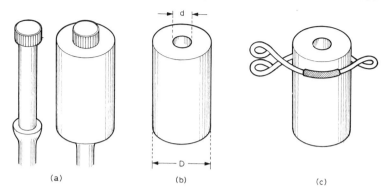

Fig. 10.4 (a) Drive spindle of a portable tape recorder with and without speed-change sleeve; the sleeve is secured by a removable thumbscrew. (b) the sleeve removed, showing internal diameter (the same as that of the drive spindle) and outside diameter. The ratio between the two gives the increase in speed. (c) the sleeve can be secured to a normal drive spindle by cutting a slot each side right through to the inside and fitting a steel wire spring.

against the drive spindle is usually not very great with battery machines because of the limited driving power, so the tape can be made to slip quite easily. With mains machines the grip is much greater, and any attempt to slow it down by this method could result in stretched or broken tape.

It could be done, though, by partially depressing the pause control, which will ease the pinch-wheel pressure. This will cause slowing if the recorder is playing, but if it is recording, it will increase the speed when the tape is played back normally. Thus, either slowing or quickening can be achieved in this way.

Another simple way to increase speed is by wrapping adhesive tape around the drive spindle, the greater the number of layers the higher the speed. When it is removed, however, ensure that every particle of adhesive is cleaned off the spindle. Methylated spirit on a piece of rag should do the trick.

Very high speeds can be achieved by running the recorder in the Fast Forward mode and bypassing the device which keeps the tape clear of the heads, if one is fitted. As the pinch wheel is not in operation, the tape can be safely slowed by hand on a mains machine. Gradual increases or decreases can be accomplished by this means if required, giving ascending or descending pitch effects.

Note that when operating in this way, it may be necessary also to neutralise any switching that mutes the amplifier circuits during Fast Wind. Another point to note is that most battery-operated recorders use d.c. motors (not all—some are impulse driven from transistor generators and tachometer-controlled) and all *simple* d.c. motor drives can be speed-changed by voltage alteration.

## Sounds Run Backwards

Another way of 'doctoring' sounds is by running them backwards. Most sounds start suddenly and die away slowly, so if this process is reversed there is a marked difference in the character of the sound. There are several ways this can be done, the easiest being to record on a 4-track machine using track 3. The tape is then turned upside down by reversing the reels and played back on a two-track model. If a 4-track recorder is not available, the recording can be made on a 2-track machine, the reels reversed, and then the tape raised in its passage across the head so that the lower part passes over the head-gap which normally reads the upper half.

The ease of this operation will depend on the model of recorder; whether there is sufficient room in front of the heads to manoeuvre the tape, and whether the tape-guides are so disposed to permit it. Some heads have guides fixed to their sides and it is difficult to alter the tape path in such a case. Where they are remote from the head it is easier. The tape displacement should be accomplished with a non-metal implement, an ideal tool being a plastics crochet-hook (Fig. 10.5).

If this method is impracticable, a reversal can be made simply by operating the pause control and then pulling the tape backward by hand but, of course, the speed will not be constant. However, it is possible to get a reasonably steady result over a short length of tape if it is pulled back evenly and carefully. Minor fluctuations will hardly be important as the intention is to distort the sound anyway.

## Wow Effect

Wow is the term used to describe a regular fluctuation of speed of a recording, and when excessive is a fault condition. It can be introduced deliberately to a sound to give the same effect as a string player adding vibrato. Sounds most affected by wow are long sustained ones and those where pitch fluctuations are not normally expected. Piano chords render wow particularly noticeable, whereas violin or woodwind notes do not. because vibrato or tremulo is normally used with them.

  The easiest way of deliberately introducing wow is by means of a layer of adhesive tape around the drive capstan, but instead of butt-joining the ends to give an even surface all around as would be done to give a straight speed increase, the ends are overlapped to give a bulge (see Fig. 10.6). An increased effect can be obtained by adding a further

layer with another overlap in the same place. There will, of course, be a
speed increase as well. Make sure that the overlap is in the opposite
direction to the rotation, otherwise the tape will tend to peel back and
get some of the adhesive on the recording tape.

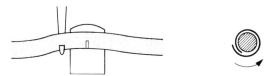

Fig. 10.5 (left) Lifting tape with a plastics crochet hook so that the gap reads the
bottom track and thus plays it backwards.

Fig. 10.6 (right) Adhesive tape wrapped around drive spindle and overlapped to
give a bulge in order to produce wow. Two layers can be used with two overlaps
in the same place to increase the effect. The tape must be wound opposite to the
direction of rotation.

## Beheading Sounds

Another interesting effect can be obtained by removing the beginning
of percussive sounds. These are sounds made by something being hit
and in musical instruments this includes the piano, xylophone, glockenspiel, drums, cymbals, triangle, etc. With musique concrete many
more percussive sounds can be used: gongs, bells, water splashing,
tins, bottles and many others.

All percussive sounds have a characteristic start of high amplitude
and suddenness, due to what are called starting transients. If these
transients are removed, the sound is completely altered in character and
in most cases is unrecognisable. Experiments with musicans have
revealed that when notes played by familiar musical instruments are
dealt with in this manner, they had difficulty in recognising them,
percussive instruments causing the greatest confusion.

The starting transients can be removed by marking the start on the
tape in the same manner as for editing, and then passing the pole of a
permanent magnet over the first half-an-inch. The magnet should be
passed vertically down over the tape, not along horizontally with a
gradual lift as this will produce a fade. Thus we will get an abrupt
cutting off of the start of the sound.

## Other Effects

Further effects can be obtained by use of the editing scissors, chopping
sounds into small sections to give rapid staccato effects, or interpolat-

Fig. 10.7    A pleasant way of combining tape recording, exercise and fresh air—making a natural sound sequence of a walk along the promenade.

ing small sections of other sounds to give rapidly alternating sandwich effects. Heavy reverberation seems to be a favourite tool of the musique concrete composer, so this can be added by the use of reverberant rooms or the empty bath technique, using a loudspeaker connected to a recorder reproducing the sound and a microphone connected to a recording recorder. These are suspended at opposite ends of a bath facing away from each other towards the wall of the bath. If further reverberation is considered desirable, the resulting recording can be replayed on the first recorder, and re-recorded on the second.

Reverberation units are now available at quite modest prices. These send the original sound along a steel spring and it is picked up at the other end together with numerous reflections that have travelled up and down the spring. The microphone is plugged into the unit which in turn is connected to the recorder. The amount of reverberation can be controlled by varying the ratio between the signal passing via the spring and a fixed amount of direct signal which bypasses the spring unit. For the serious experimenter with musique concrete, a reverberation unit would be a good investment.

### Electronic Music

Electronic music differs from musique concrete in that original signals are not derived from actual sounds but are generated from electronic sources. The equipment needed for this is complex and expensive, far out of the range of the amateur home recordist. However, as it is a form of creative recording, we will outline the basic principles.

Banks of synthesisers generate the signals. Tone generators produce sinewaves (pure tones without harmonics) at any selected frequency, which are then added to others, and harmonics of any order and in any proportion can be added. A vast number of modifications can be produced by devices known as ring modulators. Bursts of sound can have their overall wave shape modulated to conform to that of another generated frequency, and the result can undergo further and repeated modification. The signal can be altered by so many different processes that it would be almost impossible to duplicate the same sequence. Sounds can thus be created which are quite unique.

An alternative method of tone generation is derived from 'white noise', which contains every audible frequency in the same way that white light contains every visible colour. Special generators produce this white noise, then bands of frequencies can be separated out from it by electronic filters to be processed in similar manner to the single tones.

The possibilities are almost infinite, and producing a tape must be an exciting process for the dedicated enthusiast. Electronic music must not be confused with producing music from electronic instruments such as the electronic organ as this is conventional music which could be played on other keyboard instruments.

# CHAPTER ELEVEN

# RECORDING MUSIC

FROM MUSIQUE CONCRETE and electronic music we turn to music of a conventional and, for most people, a more satisfying kind. Here creativeness is not only needed in the actual performing of the music but also in the recording, as a great deal of skill and patience is needed to produce a really good result. First-class amateur music recordings are few and far between; and as any gramophone record collector will affirm, even the professionals are not always successful!

One fact that will very soon become apparent is that the recorder seems to have an uncanny knack of showing up every fault and defect. In this respect it is probably like the camera. A performance which seemed faultless when heard live at the recording session sounds very different when played back; every mistake and uneven entry seems to stand out, and at subsequent hearings seem even more obtrusive. Even performances that have no identifiable fault often sound amateurish and lack polish when heard played back. Why this should be so is not too clear, but perhaps the sight and presence of a live performance tends to distract attention from minor defects, while the concentration is greater when hearing the playback. Perhaps we are so used to hearing perfect performances from records or radio that anything that falls short is immediately obvious. Or perhaps, on hearing a performance 'the second time round' we are more critical.

This effect can be disappointing for both performers and recordist and could result in mutual recriminations! A golden rule, then, which should be applied to all amateur music-making, is not to be too ambitious. It is better to do something simple that comes off well than to attempt a difficult venture that flops, starting off with simple items that are well within the capabilities of the performers and increasing in difficulty gradually. In addition to making good recordings early on in one's experiments, the experience will be useful for the more advanced work to come later.

Simple recordings mean not only simple pieces of music, but also those that need only few performers. The greater the number of players the greater the problems of unity and ensemble, as well as problems of picking everything up on the microphones.

## Piano Accompanist

Probably the simplest venture, apart from a solo instrument, will be that of a player or singer accompanied by a piano. There may be a choice of pianists, as this is the most popular instrument, but remember that a brilliant pianist rarely makes a good accompanist. Pianists are for the most part individualists, soloists; few play well under a conductor's baton, they like to set their own pace, and many seem incapable of playing pianissimo when required!

Therefore, care should be taken in the choice of a pianist to accompany a singer or instrumentalist, and this also applies to any combination that includes a piano. Choose not the pianist with outstanding ability, but the one that will play well with others, can adjust his tempi to that of the soloist, and will not hammer out his part intent on being heard above anyone else. It is often found that a musician who plays the piano as a second instrument will make a good accompanist because he is more likely to have played with others.

## Put Performers at Ease

The fact that he is making a recording usually puts the performer under pressure, and he will tend to make more mistakes than he would if playing normally. One way of alleviating this stress is to tell the performers that several recordings are going to be made, so that the best one can be ultimately selected, or the best portions of each performance. As the bad parts will be cut out, they can be told not to worry if they make a mistake or wrong note, but to carry straight on without stopping.

This will put them more at ease as they know that a mistake will not completely ruin what was otherwise proving to be a good effort, so the chances of a mistake will be less. Some musicians, however, may be opposed to such cutting and joining of different performances, feeling that the spirit or feeling generated at any particular playing will be lost, and the result will be too clinical; perfectly played, perhaps, but without that indefinable something which performers impart to a complete uninterrupted playing of a work.

Such an argument has its point, but most commercial gramophone records are made in this way, not only lengthy sections being interposed and changed, but even short passages of a few bars. So the recordist should not feel he is cheating in some way, but that he is using every means available, in this case his editing skill, to get as flawless a performance as possible on tape. Of course, if he finds that one complete performance of the several recorded is satisfactory, this can be left as it stands as the final product.

### Piano Pitch

If a piano is included in the ensemble, this may mean a choice of several which may be available in the various homes of those involved. One factor influencing the choice will be the pitch. The majority of modern keyboard instruments are tuned to concert pitch where the middle A is set to 440Hz. Other instruments are also generally tuned to this pitch, but there are many pianos in existence which are tuned to the older 'standard pitch', a semitone lower than concert pitch.

If such an instrument is used all the others will have to tune down to it. This is not in itself difficult, especially for the strings, but instrumentalists do not like altering the pitch of their instruments as it can affect the way they behave. Singers can accept the lower pitch unless they have the rare faculty of absolute pitch, but difficulty may arise if the song reaches down to their lower register. The extra semitone may make all the difference between ease and difficulty in getting the low notes.

Pianos are occasionally found which are tuned to what used to be called 'continental pitch', which was a semitone below standard and a whole tone below concert pitch. This pitch really does create problems for the other musicians and such instruments should be avoided.

### Room Acoustics

Another factor which will need consideration is the acoustics and reverberation characteristics of the recording room. We have already dealt with the reverberation of different rooms as it affects tape dramas. The importance of a good acoustic is even greater where music is involved; with insufficient reverberation, the instruments do not seem to blend so well, and the result is thin and lacking in body.

A poor acoustic has a bad psychological effect on the musicians, who feel that their instruments are not sounding their best and unconsciously force their tone. They are thinking of how their instruments sound, rather than being immersed in the music, as they should be. On the other hand, a good acoustic, besides sounding better on the

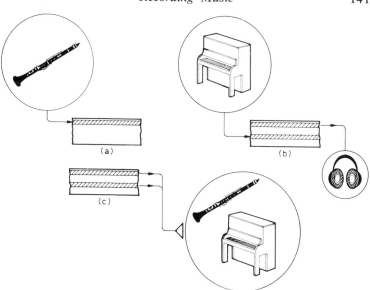

Fig. 11.1 Duoplay or sound-with-sound. (a) first step, recording made on one track. (b) second step, recording made on another track while listening to first. (c) both reproduced together by paralleling tracks.

recording, gives the musicians confidence and brings out the best in them, because it sounds good to them as they are playing.

The precise determination of individual room acoustics, and how they compare with the ideal, is quite a lengthy subject in itself. Even if accurately determined, in the case of amateur recordings in the home, domestic considerations would preclude major room modifications. However, a good rule of thumb is to select the largest room that has but few heavily upholstered items of furniture, a fair amount of wooden furniture, ample curtains at the windows, thin carpeting (not wall-to-wall) or preferably a wooden floor with a few rugs.

Heavy upholstery and carpeting absorbs high frequencies and deadens reverberation. Wooden surfaces absorb a more even range of frequencies but to a lesser extent, so these and the curtains prevent excessive reverberation and minimise room resonances which could cause certain bands of frequencies to be over-emphasised.

Some compromise will be necessary, as the room with the best acoustics may not have a piano, while the best piano lives in a room with shocking acoustics! The respective features will have to be weighed against each other, and possibly a few test recordings made to see which comes off the best. Microphone placings have been dealt with in Chapter 2.

## Duoplay

One technique that has been mentioned before, but not in detail, is that of the multiple recording. It is used mainly for musical activities and the simplest form is called *Duoplay* or *Sound-with-Sound*. A recording is made on track 1 of a 4-track recorder, then while this is being played back via a pair of headphones, another recording is made on track 3 so that both are synchronised. Finally, the two tracks can be played back together by operating the parallel-track switch on the instrument (Fig. 11.1).

Thus, the performer can do both parts; sing a duet, accompany a vocal or instrumental rendering on the piano, or play two instruments. A feature of this technique is that the tracks remain separate, and can be played separately if desired, or one can be re-made later without affecting the other. The recording can be dubbed onto a single track using another recorder if required, in the same way as making a normal copy. This method is limited to two-part recordings.

## Sound-on-Sound

Another system known as *Sound-on-Sound* is rather more complicated, but again requires a 4-track machine. The first recording is made as before on track 1. On making the next track, the first is monitored as previously with headphones, but the difference is that the recording on the first track is re-recorded on the new one along with accompanying part. This results in a recording on track 1 of one part, and a recording on track 3 consisting of both parts (Fig. 11.2).

A third part can be added by monitoring track 3 and hearing the previous two parts, while recording the third back on track 1 (this erasing the previous recording of the single part). However, the other two parts are also transferred to track 1 so that we now have all three parts on track 1 and the first two parts on track 3. A fourth, fifth and more parts can be added by alternating between tracks 1 and 3, each time transferring the recording from the old track onto the new, along with the fresh part.

The advantage here is that if a part is fluffed, all that has been done before is not spoiled because it still remains on the previous track, and we can try again as many times as we like until it is right. Of course, an earlier part cannot be corrected, only the last one, so it is necessary to make quite sure that it is satisfactory before passing on to the next part.

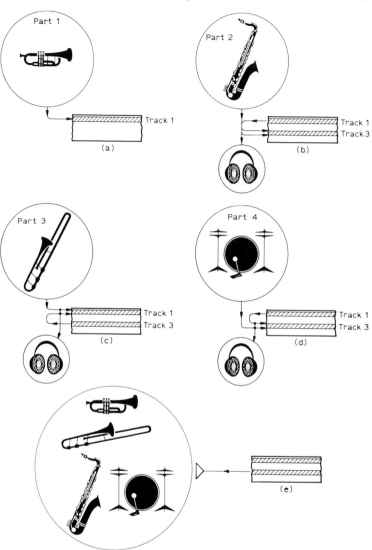

Fig. 11.2 Sound-on-sound; combining four parts. (a) part 1, trumpet recorded on track 1. (b) part 2, saxophone mixed with part 1 and the result recorded on track 3, both being monitored on the headphones. (c) part 3, trombone, mixed with the previous parts on track 3, this now being recorded on track 1, erasing part 1 thereon. Again the total result is heard in the headphones. (d) part 4, percussion, recorded on track 3 (erasing the previous recordings) together with the three parts recorded on track 1. (e) final recording on track 3, consisting of all four parts, reproduced through the loudspeaker.

Because simultaneous recording and playing back is involved in this process, a machine with two head gaps, hence a 4-track model, is essential. Furthermore, two separate internal amplifiers are also needed, and as most recorders use just a single amplifier that is switched from the record to playback mode as required, it cannot be done with a normal 4-track model. It is a built-in facility which cannot readily be added later.

With recorders that are designed for it, the process is a lot simpler than it sounds, needing only the operation of the Sound-on-Sound switch and track-switch in addition to the normal controls. The recording level of the transferred tracks is taken care of, and only the level of the new part needs to be set, as when making a normal recording.

### Sound-on-Sound with Two Recorders

Sound-on-Sound recordings can, however, be made using two 2-track recorders. The process is a little complicated as the connections are not provided internally, but it is not too difficult. First set up the two recorders and load them with tape. Record the first part in the normal way onto the first recorder, then connect the output of this machine into the radio or gram recording socket of the second, as though you were going to make a copy, and run part of the recording to set the correct level. Next, try a portion of the second part with the microphone connected to the second recorder, again in order to get the right microphone level. A pair of headphones are connected to the monitor socket of the second machine and we are ready to record the second part (Fig. 11.3).

Start the first recorder (switched to Playback) and immediately start the second (which is, of course, set to Record). Then play or sing the second part, monitoring both parts in the headphones. Thus, on the second machine, we now have a tape of both parts recorded together. If it is not satisfactory try again, because the original recording of the first part is still available on machine number 1.

A third part can then be added if required. A lead is connected from the second recorder output to the gram socket of the first, the microphone is plugged into the first and the headphones into the monitor. Again check on the levels for both microphone and gram input and then record part three, hearing the total result on the phones. For part four, once more reverse the connections, playing back the product so far on machine 1 and recording it together with part four on machine 2 and monitoring there from. As many parts as required can be added as with a proper Sound-on-Sound four-track machine.

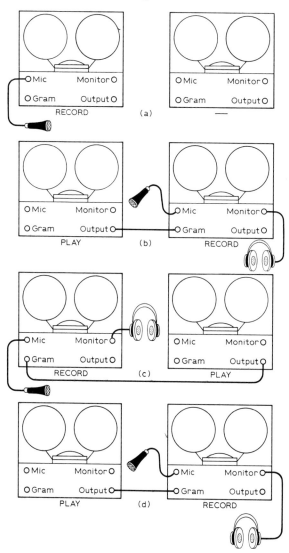

Fig. 11.3 Multiple recording using two standard 2-track recorders. (a) Recording part 1 on first machine. (b) Connect output of first recorder to gram socket of second recorder. Play part 1 and record it on second recorder together with part 2, with headphones connected to monitor socket on second recorder so that both parts can be heard. (c) Connect output of second recorder to gram socket of first. Connect microphone to first recorder and record the third part on it together with previous parts played back from second recorder. Headphone monitor first recorder. (d) Connect as in (b), enabling fourth part to be recorded.

One advantage of using two recorders is that each step need not be erased as succeeding steps can be recorded further along the tape, which cannot be done with a Sound-on-Sound 4-track recorder. Thus, if any part is unsatisfactory, it is unnecessary to start again from the beginning, simply going back to the point where that part was added, and taking it from there. As there is a permanent record of how the tape was made up from the various parts, it might be interesting to include them all in the final product, but remember that alternate steps are on two separate tapes on the two machines, so they will have to be edited into one.

Fig. 11.4    It is sometimes necessary to use more than one microphone to obtain the best results. In this photograph a Beyer M260 unidirectional ribbon microphone is being used for the voice and a Beyer M160 double ribbon unit for the instrument.

Fig. 11.5 Making a multiple recording. Left—the violin part is recorded first. Right—the violin part recorded on the first machine is being fed into the second tape recorder which is also recording the piano part. The result is being monitored on headphones to ensure synchronisation.

## Speed and Pitch

It may be thought that time could be saved by not changing all the connections and level settings at each step, but instead transpose the tapes, so that machine 1 is always recording and machine 2 playing. This sounds feasible, but no two machines run at exactly the same speed. Assuming that machine 2 runs slower than machine 1 by $1\frac{1}{2}\%$, which is not excessive, the first part recorded on machine 1 will be about an eighth of a tone lower when played back on machine 2. The result recorded with part two on machine 1 when played again on machine 2, will then be a quarter tone down, and part two an eighth. The result is therefore cumulative, with each part being separated from the next by an eighth of a tone, and with four parts, the first and last will be a semitone apart.

The result can be well imagined! Even with smaller speed differences, the cumulative effect will give a noticeable difference in pitch between the first and last where several parts are thus recorded. It is therefore important that the playback must be on the same machine that made the recording, even though this entails changing the leads and resetting the levels.

## Cueing In

All the parts must start precisely together otherwise the effect will be ragged. The best way of cueing is to count either a complete bar or part of it into the microphone when making the first part, then come in on the appropriate beat. This count-in will be heard in the headphones with all successive parts, and can be edited out or erased with a magnet when the recording is completed.

When setting the recording levels of the microphone and the tape of the previous parts individually before each step, remember that they will both be recorded together, hence the level will be higher than that of each one separately. This should be allowed for by setting the levels at about half or two-thirds of the normal position. It will not be possible to alter it while performing, so set it slightly low if in doubt. Automatic controls should not be used, although one may be tempted to do so if the facility exists, as these reduce the dynamic range of the recording, and while useful for some applications, are not desirable for music.

## Distortion

In theory, the number of parts that can be added are without limit, but in practice, with ordinary domestic tape recorders, this is not the case. Each time a recording is made, a slight amount of distortion is added. This is small, so that it would be difficult to distinguish a copy from an original if the machine is in good condition, but after four or five recordings, the distortion begins to add up into an audible effect.

Distortion can be minimised by always recording at the fastest speed, even if the final recording is needed at a lower one. Wow and flutter, which are different types of speed irregularities, will also be less at the higher speed. At medium and low speeds, a certain amount of treble boost is given to a recording to compensate for the falling high frequency response; this too will be cumulative, so that at each re-recording the same band of frequencies will be boosted further. After several steps, the original will take on a distinctly edgey sound with transients being over-emphasised. At the faster speed, the amount of boost is less, so this effect will be at least, reduced.

The recording distortion shows up worse on instruments with a large number of natural harmonics, such as the violin and clarinet. As the earlier parts will be most distorted from successive re-recordings, instruments that are least affected, i.e. those with fewer harmonics and lower pitch, should be recorded first. The melody or lead part is the most prominent, so this should be given the least distortion by being recorded last if possible.

Fig. 11.6 A music mixer designed and built by the author. It has twelve independent channels and twenty-four microphone inputs for orchestra and choir which can be faded relative to each other without disturbing individual channel settings.

There may be other considerations arising out of the music itself which may modify this order. With four-part harmony, the melody and the bass are often the most prominent, with the inner harmonies of alto and tenor being less so. These could be recorded first, then the bass, and finally the melody part. A pizzicato bass or rhythm drum part would not suffer too much from distortion, so these could be recorded first. These notes on distortion apply both to sound-on-sound recorders as well as the two-recorder set up, because successive recordings are made in each case.

Recordings of live music, either straight or multiple, pose many problems but while it is true that many amateur music recordings turn out less than successful, there are also those that prove very good. Patience is needed, and attention to the several points outlined here, but above all do not become too ambitious at first. Keep well within the capabilities of the performers and there is no reason why very satisfying recorded performances should not result.

# CHAPTER TWELVE

# RECORDING IN STEREO

THE PRINCIPLE OF STEREO is quite simple, although the technicalities are not. We hear sounds from many directions, and are able to distinguish them by reason of having two ears. Numerous factors are involved in our aural reaction to these sounds; one ear will hear them a little later than the other, there will be differences of volume level, and the shielding effect of the head and external formation of the ear will cause subtle differences which enables the brain to identify the direction of the sound source.

### Theory of Stereo

Stereo attempts to duplicate this effect, although imperfectly. Two microphones or sets of microphones pick up sound to the left and right respectively; these are processed through completely separate channels to be reproduced by two loudspeakers positioned to the left and right of the listener. The effect is that we hear sounds coming from the extreme left and right together with an illusion of sound coming from the centre and other intermediate points. Thus we create a spread of sound between the loudspeakers.

The reason for this effect is that like the ears, the two microphones both receive the same sounds, but with delays and level differences, and these are passed on eventually to the two ears of the listener via the loudspeakers. Thus a sound coming from the right will be predominantly in the right-hand channel, but there will be also traces of it in the left, much weaker and composed to a large extent of reverberations, and coming slightly later. A central sound source will give equal signals in level and timing, and the sound will appear to come from between the loudspeakers. Other positions will give varying proportions and delays to the two channels.

To record stereo, we must have a recorder that will record two channels simultaneously, and of course play them back. Many of the more expensive models are designed for stereo recording. Usually they

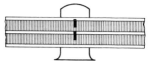

Fig. 12.1 A 4-track stereo head reading a 2-track tape. The bottom track only partially coincides with the bottom head gap.

are of the 4-track variety, thus enabling four mono recordings or two stereo recordings to be made on each tape, but there are also some that use only two tracks, giving a single stereo recording to each tape.

It should be noted that the two are not compatible. Pre-recorded stereo music tapes are available, and some of these are 2-track recordings. A 4-track machine will not 'read' the tracks correctly; reference to Fig. 12.1 shows that although the top track is more or less in a position to cover the top head-gap, the bottom one only partially covers it. Thus, the output from the bottom channel will be weak and noisy.

However, our interest is in *making* stereo recordings, so obviously the playback will be on the same machine that made the recording, hence we should not experience such difficulties.

## Microphone Positions

There are two main methods of microphone positioning. The first, which is favoured in this country and in Europe, is to have the two microphones mounted in a single unit, but pointing at an angle to left and right (Fig. 12.2a); most stereo microphones sold here are of this style.

The other method, used a lot in America, is to mount the two microphones completely separately at some distance from each other (Fig. 12.2b). Both methods have their devotees and their advantages. In the case of the single unit it is argued that a more natural effect will be achieved because the configuration is close to that of the human ears, thus the microphones will receive sound much as the ears of a listener would in the same position. On the other hand, it is argued that spaced

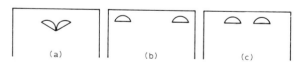

Fig. 12.2 (a) Single unit stereo microphone consisting of two angled elements. (b) Two remote microphones for stereo recording. (c) Compromise arrangement with closely spaced microphones to minimise the disadvantages of methods (a) and (b).

microphones simulate the position of the reproducing loudspeakers and therefore the speakers will be radiating the same sound from the same position from which the microphones received it.

Both have their points and their snags. Take the case of a voice coming from the extreme right or left. The single-unit microphone, being in the centre of proceedings, will be several feet away, but the further away from a microphone the sound source is, the greater will be the proportion of reverberation. Thus there will be a high degree of reverberation, giving a distant effect to the voice. This will sound unnatural when coming from a loudspeaker in the approximate position of the original voice. On the other hand, a voice from the *centre* would have a similar distant reverberant sound when picked up by *spaced* microphones.

There is, therefore, an argument for using a different system for different recordings. Those having a small stereo spread, such as a conversation between two or three people close together, could use the single unit, while those spread over a larger area could make use of spaced microphones. Some of the stereo microphones made for use as a stacked unit can be separated if needed and used spaced. A compromise is to space the microphones 3–4 feet apart so that both centre and extreme side positions would not be too far from a microphone and therefore introduce too much reverberation. Good results can be obtained from this method.

A useful dodge that can be used in a tape drama is to alter the microphone positions from one scene to the next, not only relative to each other, but also to their locations in the room. The consequent change of ambience will emphasise the change of scene. Tape dramas will be complicated by the use of stereo, because in addition to dialogue, cues and effects directions, the script must contain information on performers positions like a stage play. The actors will have to occupy the positions specified in the script, and move about during the action. This must be done without too much extraneous noise.

## Stereo Sound Effects

If it is intended to purchase a stereo recorder and concentrate on stereo recordings, the sound effects collection will have to be largely in stereo, which may not be easy to achieve. Many of the sources of effects outlined in Chapter 7 will be in mono only, and outdoor effects will have to be in mono unless a portable stereo recorder is also obtained.

It may be possible to get some stereo recordings on location with the mains machine if facilities are available. For example, recordings of passing traffic (always more dramatic in stereo) could be made from the window of a friend's house near a main road. A thunderstorm is also most impressive in stereo, and can be recorded from one's own home.

However, even if many stereo effects prove unattainable, stereo can sometimes be simulated from mono sources. Take a single sound of short duration, such as breaking glass; this mono effect can be fed into the right hand or left hand channel to give a directional effect on playback, or fed to both channels equally to give a central playback effect.

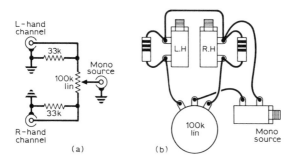

Fig. 12.3 (a) Theroretical diagram of stereo direction control. (b) Wiring diagram, viewed from back, showing connection of components.

The position can also be adjusted between these extremes or even made to move across the stereo-image area by varying the proportions fed to the two channels. This can be done by a Stereo Direction Control, a simple piece of equipment which can be made by anyone who can make a few soldered joints (see Fig. 12.3a). Three jack sockets are needed, one for each channel on the stereo recorder and one for the mono effects recorder, although the leads could be wired into the control unit thus saving the cost of the sockets and plugs. The control is effected by means of a potentiometer (100kΩ linear track) mounted at the front of the box containing the device and fitted with a large pointer-knob. Fig. 12.3b shows the practical wiring of the unit; the positions of the resistors and sockets are not critical.

If the knob is fitted so that it points at equal angles from the upright at the two extremes of its travel, it will indicate the direction from which the sound will appear; maximum left will make the sound come from the extreme left, maximum right from the extreme right, and upright will give a centre source. Some effects such as footsteps can be made to 'walk' from one side to the other by turning the control in the required direction.

This is not true stereo, of course, because there will not be the slight time delays and ambience effects which are needed to make it really authentic. However, a very realistic stereo simulation can be made which will give some sense of direction to the sounds.

### Recording and Editing

If genuine stereo effects are recorded, and these later prove to be the wrong way round for the production in hand, they can be simply reversed by changing the connections to the stereo recorder, the left hand to the right and vice-versa.

As well as script complications referred to earlier, the managing of the actual recording and mixing in of effects (tricky at the best of times with a tape drama) becomes more complex. It really needs two operators, one directing, by giving cue signals and managing the actors, and the other looking after the effects. It is advisable to get some experience with mono productions before embarking on stereo.

As the two tracks of a stereo recording are directly above and in line with each other, there is no special problem when it comes to editing. The techniques described for mono editing apply equally to stereo.

### Playback

For best playback effect, the loudspeakers should be spaced to give an equal-sided triangle between them and the listener. Most stereo recorders have detachable speakers which can be positioned wherever convenient. Some speakers are permanently connected by their flex, others by means of non-reversible plugs and sockets. If the connections have to be remade, ensure that they are the same as they were before; if

Fig. 12.4 Two mains-operated stereo tape recorders. Left—Beocord 2400 with slider-type controls. Right—Ferrograph *Series Seven* which incorporates Dolby B noise-reduction system.

Fig. 12.5   Two more stereo tape recorders. Left—Brennell Mk6. Right—Victor MTR12ME which is designed for 4-channel quadrasonic recording and playback.

one speaker connection is reversed, the cones will be out of phase, one moving back while the other is moving forward, instead of moving in the same direction. This will cause partial sound cancellation and inferior results. The stereo image will be confused, and the lower tones will sound weak and thin.

If there is any doubt about the speaker phasing, it can be checked by a simple sound test. Play over a musical tape which has plenty of bass, and stand the speakers side by side. After listening carefully for a few moments, reverse the connections to one speaker only, and listen again. In one position, the bass will be thin and poor, while in the other it will be normal. Leave the connections to give the normal bass.

## Creative Possibilities

Undoubtedly, the tape drama is literally given an extra dimension by stereo. To locate characters and sounds adds greatly to the interest, and helps to convey the action, which is not always easy by non-visual means. Stereo opens up many exciting possibilities as plot developments can be used that need directional sound sources and would otherwise be difficult to make clear. The extra complexity, once mastered, should be more than repaid by the enlarged scope.

Sound sequences are also enhanced by stereo, especially story sequences, but as they consist entirely of sound effects, and stereo effects are not so easy to obtain, this may pose problems. Similarly because they convey incidents and events, impressionist and natural sequences will benefit from stereo, though perhaps to a lesser extent; as

F

these involve recording outdoors, a portable stereo machine would be essential.

Musique concrete is an interesting case. Although true stereo would be difficult to achieve, some fascinating effects can be obtained with simulated stereo. Examples include staccato sounds jumping rapidly from left to right, or slower answering effects, sliding or glissando sounds gliding from one side to the other, circling and hovering. Much could be done here to add interest and increase creative scope by using direction, by means of the stereo direction control.

What about interviews? Since these consist of just one person talking (even the interviewer is cut out in the editing process) there is little to be gained by recording in stereo. Because most interviews are on-the-spot affairs, a stereo portable machine would be required. We have seen, too, that the microphone can be off-putting to some subjects, hence the need to make it inconspicuous. Stereo microphones are anything but inconspicuous, and very likely would frighten many interviewees into tongue-tied silence. Mono is really the most suitable medium for this field.

Music is what most people think of when stereo is mentioned. Realism and presence is certainly added, but whether this really adds to the value of the music is debatable. Trick effects as with musique concrete are not needed (or in fact desirable); just a pair of microphones positioned to give a distinguishable left and right-hand channel effect. It is certainly worth trying, however, to decide whether the result is enhanced by the use of stereo.

### Stereo from Mono Recorders

It is possible to make stereo recordings with two mono machines, but there are many snags. In theory all that is required is to run two recorders with their microphones at the same time, one as the left hand and the other as the right hand channel. The difficulties arise in synchronising them, as they must keep in step to a fraction of a second right to the end of the recording. No two recorders have precisely the same speed, so the resulting tapes (two would always be required, another inconvenience) would always have to be played on the same machines and no others.

However, even the same recorder will not keep to *exactly* the same speed from day to day. If the weather is warm or the machine has been warmed up well, the oil and lubricants will give less drag than when cold. Fluctuations of mains voltage will produce torque variations in the motor, and although the motor is supposed to run at a constant speed determined by the mains frequency, it will slow if the torque is reduced and the load is heavy, i.e. when starting from cold. Minute

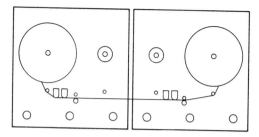

Fig. 12.6    Two mono 4-track recorders arranged in tandem to record stereo. Tape drive must be by the right-hand recorder only.

layers of dirt on the drive capstan will cause very slight speed increases.

Permutations of these and other small variations can lead to very noticeable errors, so that two recorders that kept in step during a recording would probably never finish at the same place simultaneously again. Even a 0·1% difference in speed between them means a difference of *3·6 seconds* in an hour!

There is also the difficulty of starting the two recorders at precisely the same moment. Mark both tapes with splicing tape and line these starting marks up with the heads. The machines should have been switched on for at least five minutes or more, and the tape held by the pause control. Releasing both pause controls at the same time should give a good start and ensure reasonable synchronism. A check could be included, by recording a short sudden sound such as a hand clap at the start. If two are heard on playback, a false start is indicated.

**Recorders in Tandem**

Another possibility, but which presents practical difficulties, is to set up two 4-track recorders side by side with the heads and the spools of the two machines in line horizontally. A tape is loaded onto the left-hand machine, and threaded across its heads in the normal way. It is then taken over to the right-hand recorder, passed over its heads and slotted into its take-up spool (Fig. 12.6). The first recorder is switched to track 1 and the second to track 3.

It would not be possible to have both capstans driving the tape, because of speed differences. If the first one was slightly fast, tape would become slack between the two instruments and start to pile up on the table; if the second was fast, then the tape would be stretched and probably break. Drive must be by one recorder only (the second, right-hand one) so this means that the drive on the other must be neutralised.

This can be done on some recorders by merely locking the pause control in the off position so that the pinch wheel is held off from the capstan, allowing the tape to pass through at a speed determined by the second instrument. Normally, however, brakes are applied to the spools by the pause control, and if (as is often the case) they are only lightly applied in the pause position, the resistance offered by the paying out spool will keep the tape taut. If braking is firm, however, the drag will be too heavy and cause slow running and tape stretching. The braking can be judged by turning the left-hand turntable by hand to assess the drag.

If the drag is too great, the instrument must be operated in the normal running position, but with the pinch wheel held off from the drive spindle in some way. No damage will be inflicted as the pinch-wheel arm is spring-loaded. Just how it can be done depends on the layout of the tape-deck and the ingenuity of the operator; a specially-made bracket supported against a pillar or guide, or even a loop of cord could do the trick.

Using the two microphones as a stereo pair, the signals will not be recorded immediately one above the other, but will be spaced along the tape by the distance between the two record heads. Thus editing will not be possible. Furthermore, when playing back, the same spacing must be arranged, and the easiest way of doing this is to make sure that the recorders are actually touching each other side-to-side both during recording and playback.

It is advisable to use external speakers for the playback, because the internal speakers will be too close together to give good stereo. The method is rather ungainly, but it can be made to work.

## Quadrasonics

Stereo changes the single-dimensional monophonic sound to that of two dimensions, spreading it out before the listener as though on a stage. Quadraphonics (or Quadrasonics), as the name implies, features four main sound sources, adding the rear and the front to the left and right of conventional stereo, so that the listener is surrounded by sound, hence the name sometimes used—'surround stereo'.

(Note: the author feels that *Quadrasonics*, from the Latin "four sounds", is preferable to the hybrid Latin/Greek term *Quadraphonics*, although the latter seems to be gaining favour at the time of writing).

Four separate channels are used, each with its own amplifier and loudspeaker, two speakers being positioned at the front in the conventional stereo location, and two at the rear. Complete integrated amplifiers are now being produced with four channels, as are quadrasonic gramophone records. Whether this will be the successor to 2-track stereo remains to be seen; certainly there are many difficulties in getting four channels on a disc and designing a successful pickup to play it. There are no such problems with tape, as all that is needed is a head with four gaps.

What, then, is the effect on the listener for the various types of programme material? For drama and sound-sequences, to have some of the action apparently taking place behind you, is rather disconcerting, and there is a natural tendency to turn the head to see what is happening. From earliest times, plays and dramatic presentations have been displayed in *front* of the audience; to have the audience sited as though in the middle of the action can be confusing.

A modification of the system is to bring the rear speakers to the sides of the listener, perhaps just a little forward, and the two front speakers a little closer together and further forward from the listeners. The four speakers would thus describe an arc of about 160° in front of the listener. This should give a forward depth and extended image right out to the sides. Of course, the microphones in the original recording would have to occupy the same positions.

## Music in Quad

Music can be treated in two ways quadrasonically. A small group of instruments can be placed partly in front and partly behind the listener. Thus he is surrounded by the musicians as though in the middle of the

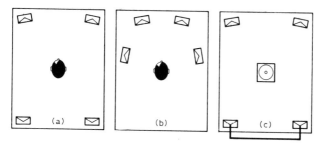

Fig. 12.7   (a) Quadrophony, using four channels and loudspeakers to provide sounds from the rear as well as the front. (b) An arrangement probably more satisfactory for tape dramas, which has no rear sound but greater depth forward. (c) A variant for music in which two rear loudspeakers are fed from one channel, the fourth feeding an overhead loudspeaker to simulate reverberation from walls and roof.

group. Many demonstrations of quadrasonics have used this mode, but the result, although realistic, is not musically satisfactory. No one when attending a concert, or having a musical evening at home with friends, would insist on sitting in the middle of the group of musicians! As with the early days of stereo, probably more people have been put off by ill-conceived demonstrations than won over.

A second way of recording music quadrasonically is to have the musicians spread out in front of the listener as with two-channel stereo, the rear speakers reproducing just the echoes and reverberations that would come from behind in a concert hall. In favourable conditions this adds a spaciousness and gives the impression of being actually in the hall, improving the flatter image produced by two-channel stereo. Whether this really adds anything of value to the music itself is another matter.

As the reverberations from the back of the hall will be very little different from either side, the two rear channels could be replaced by a single unit, feeding two speakers if desired. The fourth channel could then be used to feed an overhead speaker. Reverberations coming from the roof of a concert hall would be quite different in nature from those coming from the rear wall, and these could be conveyed by a ceiling-mounted speaker. Again, the recording microphones would have to be in the appropriate positions. This could well give a more realistic effect, if that is what is required, than using the four channels in the conventional manner.

It can be seen, then, that there is constant technical development in the field of sound recording and much scope for interesting experiment by the well-equipped amateur.

CHAPTER THIRTEEN

# FAULTS AND MAINTENANCE

Tape recorders, like any other mechanisms, need periodic maintenance to keep them in good running order. Failure to do so may not always precipitate a total breakdown, but performance will be degraded, and so much effort and skill which may have been put into making creative tape recordings will be nullified by inferior results.

## Head Cleaning

The main requirement is to keep clean the path over which the tape passes, particularly the record and playback heads. Loose oxide from the tape tends to accumulate on the front of the heads, and build up a hard deposit. If the head magnetic gap, which is normally filled with non-magnetic material, becomes worn and develops a cavity (as it often does after prolonged use) this serves as a key which retains the oxide.

Periodic cleaning is therefore required, depending on the amount of use given the machine, the tape used (some tapes shed their oxide more readily than others) and the heads (some heads permit oxide to build up more quickly than others). A quick visual examination will usually indicate whether cleaning is required, but after prolonged use, it is as well to clean the heads whether there is a visible oxide deposit or not.

Various tools are available to perform head cleaning, and there are special tapes that can be soaked in cleansing solution and run through the machine like a recording tape. However, from experience in a professional workshop it has been found that the most effective method is by means of a simple home-made tool, consisting of an ice-lolly stick tapered to about a quarter of an inch wide at the bottom, to which is glued a quarter-inch-square of felt. The felt should not be more than $\frac{1}{8}''$ thick otherwise it will be impossible to get it down between the head and the pressure-pad in some models (a fault with at least one of the commercial head-cleaning tools).

Keep a small bottle of methylated-spirit with a screw stopper, for cleaning. Pour some into the stopper, dip the tool into it and apply the felt to the face of the heads, rubbing to remove any visible deposits. Dip the tool in the stopper again to clean the felt and apply once more to the heads, repeating again to make sure the faces are quite clean. The faces can then be polished off with another similar tool kept dry for the purpose. The remaining spirit in the stopper, being contaminated with oxide, can then be thrown away; the spirit in the bottle must not be spoiled by dipping the tool directly into it.

Fig. 13.1 (left) Periodic cleaning of the tape head is necessary for the best results. This *Bib* kit contains tape head cleaning fluid, applicators, tape head polishers and a cleaning cloth.

Fig. 13.2 (right) A kit of cleaning fluids, applicators, brush, lubricants and a stroboscope.

## Pinchwheel, Guides and Pressure Pads

Other parts of the tape path which should be similarly cleaned are the guides, the drive spindle and the rubber pinch wheel. The drive spindle is especially important as any deposits here will cause speed fluctuations. Powdered oxide and fluff can be cleaned out of the space around the heads by means of a small brush or by using a blower. The felt pressure pads should be inspected and should be soft with no trace of hardness or caked oxide. If this is not so, they can be improved by rubbing the felt surface with a nail file, ensuring not to poke or scratch the face of the head while so doing.

Fig. 13.3   With well used tapes an improvement can often be made by bulk erasing as in the example shown (Leeraser 70 Tape Demagnetizer).

## Demagnetising

It is necessary to periodically demagnetise the heads. Over a period, the heads become slightly magnetised and tapes played with the heads in this condition can become noisy. Demagnetising is effected by applying a strong alternating magnetic field, and gradually reducing it until it dies away. A demagnetiser (or defluxer) consists of an electromagnet operated from the mains supply; the poles are applied to the front of the head to produce a strong 50Hz field at the face. The device is then slowly moved away and switched off.

Another method of defluxing uses the bias and erase oscillations generated inside the recorder. These are applied to the heads during normal use, but when the Stop key is operated they are switched off immediately. Head defluxing can be accomplished by simply switching the recorder to Record, and then pulling the mains plug out. The oscillations will not cease immediately, but will die away as the valves cool and the capacitors discharge. With transistor recorders, high-value reservoir and smoothing capacitors take a few seconds to discharge, thus giving a slow decay of the oscillation. This method cannot be applied to battery instruments unless there is a large-value decoupling capacitor across the battery supply. Heavily magnetised heads should be defluxed with a demagnetiser but self-defluxing, if carried out regularly, will prevent the magnetisation from building up to a level which needs more drastic treatment.

It should be noted that whole tapes can be wiped clean by a bulk eraser in a matter of seconds without having to run them through the recorder. The principle is similar to the head defluxer. It can be useful, but is not normally necessary because, of course, previous recordings are erased when new ones are made.

**Head Wear**

After several years' use the head becomes worn, and eventually needs replacing, a flat channel the width of the tape appearing across the head face. If the wear is even over the area of the channel, there is little effect on performance, but usually the edges of the gap become distorted and rounded, and sometimes the non-magnetic filler disappears, leaving a cavity which quickly fills up with oxide from the tape, necessitating frequent cleaning. Enlargement of the gap results in a drop in the upper frequency response.

Determination of when to replace the head must be decided by the appearance of the head-face and the frequency response. If in doubt, make a recording involving considerable high transient sounds, such as jangling a bunch of keys, then check if the upper response is impaired. If course, if one waits until deterioration becomes really noticeable, all recent recordings will be affected, so it is wise to replace before it gets really bad.

The erase head is not so important; quite severe wear can be seen but it will still perform its function of erasing previous recordings. This is because the size of the head gap does not materially affect the erasing process. Only rarely will it be necessary to change this component.

Replacing the record/playback head is usually a straightforward job, but rather delicate soldering is involved requiring a miniature soldering iron and some soldering skill. Wires must be resoldered to the same connections on the new head, which should be of the same type as the original head. Do not hold the iron on the work longer than necessary to make a good joint, and ensure that the iron does not damage the insulation on other wires.

**Adjusting the Head Azimuth**

It is important for the gap in the head to be perfectly upright. If this is not so, the vertical magnetic zones that have been recorded on the tape will be bridged across the gap as shown in Fig. 13.4 and the effective width of the gap increased resulting in a reduced high-frequency response. This applies to tapes that have been recorded on a machine with a vertical gap but played back on one where the gap is not vertical.

If a tape is recorded on a machine with an off-vertical R/P head and played back on a machine with an upright gap, the effect will be as shown at Fig. 13.4b. The magnetic zones will be at the same angle as the gap in the recording machine, and therefore an upright gap will bridge them, also leading to high-frequency loss.

The only time when optimum frequency response can be achieved with a non-vertical head-gap is when the recording and playback gap is

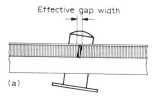
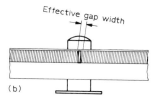

Fig. 13.4 (a) A head gap off vertical bridges several high frequency magnetized stripes on the tape. Thus its effective width is increased with the consequent loss of high frequency response. (b) A similar effect is obtained when a tape recorded on a machine with an off-vertical gap is played back on one that is vertical.

at the same angle, in other words when the recording is played back on the same machine. Therefore, to ensure that recordings are compatible with other machines, it is essential that the head is positioned to give a vertical gap, or azimuth setting.

To facilitate this, the record head is mounted so that it can be rocked from side to side and locked in the correct position. Fig. 13.5 illustrates a commonly-used method. A ridge runs from front to back at the bottom of the head and the head is secured by two screws, one on each side. The azimuth setting is adjusted by first screwing both screws down but not too tight. Then one screw is unscrewed while the other is screwed up by an equal amount, thus causing the head to tilt over the ridge. This is done until the correct setting is found and then both are tightened to lock the head in that position. If they are overtightened the flanges will bend or break.

Two small screwdrivers are needed for this operation, so that the screws can be turned simultaneously in opposite directions. Some heads have only one adjusting screw, the tension being maintained by means of a spring. One version of this arrangement is shown in Fig. 13.5b. Therefore when replacing a head carefully note the positions of

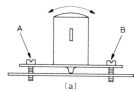
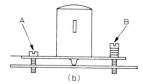

Fig. 13.5 (a) Head azimuth is adjusted by turning screws A and B in opposite directions; this tilts the head over the ridge in its base. (b) Single screw adjustment is afforded by turning screw A. Screw B is fixed but is fitted with a coil-spring to maintain tension.

springs, washers, etc. and replace them in reverse order. To avoid magnetising the heads, use a brass screwdriver for the job.

## Test Tape

Professionally, the adjustment is made by means of special test tapes with high-frequency tones recorded on them. Fairly accurate adjustment can be made without these and the amateur recordist can with care adjust the azimuth himself, as he will need to do when replacing a head.

To do this, make a recording (on a machine known to have its azimuth set correctly) of a steady sound containing a lot of high frequencies. Sustained applause is very good for this purpose, as clapping produces high transient content. Hissing of escaping gas or air could also be used. No doubt there will be something suitable on the effects tape.

On replaying the tape on the machine to be adjusted, the sound will be dull and muffled if the azimuth is offset, but as the head is adjusted to one side and approaches the correct setting, crispness and clarity increases. An optimum position will be reached where clarity will be greatest, then it will decrease again as the head passes out of the vertical in the opposite direction. The adjustment is swung either side of the optimum, each time reducing the overshoot, finally arriving at the best position.

If the azimuth optimum cannot be found in one direction, the head must be tilted in the opposite direction until it is found. When tightening the screws in the two-screw adjustment arrangement, be careful to see that the head does not move out of the true position. Tighten both equally, while the test tape is still playing, and listen for any decrease in clarity. Rather than overtighten, it is best to do as the manufacturers do, put a blob of paint on the screw head, to secure it in the right position.

These are the points of maintenance and adjustment that need to be done from time to time. Once the azimuth is set it should not need touching unless the head is replaced or disturbed. However, sometimes the gap can wear to an irregular contour, and a slightly different azimuth setting can improve the response. But, if things get as bad as that the head should be replaced anyway.

## Common Faults: Weak Sound

The most common fault is weak and muffled sound. Previously-made recordings are usually not too bad, but recordings made with the faulty machine sound the worst, sometimes being almost inaudible. In nearly every case the cause is a dirty record head, and cleaning will clear the trouble. Even if the head appears to be normal, it should be cleaned before going any further, as a few grains of oxide, almost invisible, can play havoc if they lodge across the gap. If the head is quite clean, head wear may be responsible. Again, a visual examination will determine this; note that deterioration takes place slowly so that any sudden symptom of this nature is unlikely to be caused by head wear.

Low volume and poor h.f. response can also be caused when the tape does not make intimate contact with the recording head. The pressure pad provided to ensure such contact can sometimes become displaced, detached from its carrier, or the carrier may become stuck, thus giving rise to the symptom. Refitting the pad or freeing the carrier will restore normal working.

A surprising number of beginners are caught out by threading a tape to the take-up spool with the shiny side inwards. When it is rewound and played back, the oxide side is not in contact with the head and playback is quiet and muffled. Many modern tapes have the oxide surface polished to reduce head wear, so it is not always easy to distinguish one from the other, although the oxide side will always be a little duller than the outside surface. It is not unknown for machines to be returned to the maker's service department with nothing wrong other than the tape being reversed!

### Incomplete Erasure

Another fault often encountered is incomplete erasure, the old recording being heard in the background of the new one. The most likely cause is dirt on the erase head, and cleaning should be the first step. A fault in the track switch with a 4-track recorder can prevent the erase current from reaching the head, as can a broken lead. The latter is not likely unless the leads have been disturbed.

The next suspect is the oscillator circuit that produces the erase current. As this also supplies recording bias to the record head, a failure of this circuit should also produce severe distortion. Locating and repairing the precise fault is a job for the experts. Sometimes the oscillator will generate sufficient power to provide bias but not enough to give complete erasure, hence the quality is not noticeably affected, but there will be partial erasure only, the old recording being just audible in the background.

The erase head can also develop a fault causing similar symptoms and professional advice will be needed. If the heads have recently been disturbed, or the recorder has been in an accident, the erase head may be out of alignment. It must be in line with the record head so that its gap follows the same path, otherwise it will erase only part of the track. With some recorders the height of the heads is adjustable, and the correct position is with the top of the gap just below the top edge of the tape. The erase head azimuth setting is not important.

## Distortion

Distortion has many causes. Lack of recording bias is common, although this will usually be accompanied by no (or partial) erasure. The feed circuit from oscillator to record head could be faulty, causing lack of bias, with normal erasure. To test for this condition, try a previously recorded tape. If the quality is normal, the distortion is only taking place during recording and so the bias is the chief suspect.

If there is distortion on both recording and playback (the former can be heard over the monitor) or on playback only, the trouble is in the amplifier and it requires the attention of the service engineer.

## Hum

Hum can be a great problem. Determine whether it is taking place during recording or playback, by switching to Playback with no tape. Excessive hum on playback (there will always be a small residual hum, especially with the volume turned well up) could be due to a broken lead at the record head.

If there is an earth lead in the mains cable and this is connected to the third pin of the mains plug, hum can be produced. The mains earth wires run for a considerable distance in close proximity to the power wires and they can pick up hum from them. Try disconnecting the earth lead in the plug, also try reversing the two supply leads, as sometimes it will be found that there is less hum one way round than the other. However, hum on playback is usually due to amplifier trouble, most likely a faulty smoothing capacitor in the power supply circuit, and the service engineer should be consulted.

If the playback of previously recorded tapes is satisfactory, the hum is taking place during recording, and the most likely trouble is the microphone or its lead, or the direct recording lead. Hum on record can be heard in the monitor, or seen on the modulation indicator. When the level control is turned up, the indicator will show a steady reading even when no sound being picked up by the microphone; unplugging the microphone or any other input lead will stop the indication. Check the connections in the plug, and if everything seems in order, cut off about three inches of cable and reconnect the plug. Cable breaks often occur an inch or so from the plug and are not seen because they are covered with the insulation. If there is still hum, the trouble must be at the microphone end of the cable.

## Complete Failure

Failure to function at all can be due to a break in the mains cable, usually near the plug, or a broken connection in the plug or perhaps a blown fuse. There should be some indication as to where these are fitted, although not all recorders have them. If the mains circuit is at fault, both the motor and the amplifier will be dead. As it is unlikely that there would be a fault in both the amplifier and motor at the same time, it can be safely concluded that mains circuit troubles are present if both fail. If one functions, mains faults are ruled out.

## Wow

Common faults with tape recorders are those affecting the tape transport system. Being purely mechanical, they are more prone to trouble than the electrical circuits. Speed variations are the most usual: either wow (the regular rise and fall of pitch) or flutter (fluctuations often too rapid to individually distinguish them).

The source of wow can best be discovered by comparing the frequency of the pitch variations with the speed of the various rotating members. Thus a pitch variation coinciding with a single rotation of one of the spools would indicate that the spool or something associated with it is the cause. If the cheeks of the spool are warped, they may rub against part of the tape-deck thus causing a slowing down once per revolution; alternatively, the tape may be fouling against one of the cheeks.

A faster variation should be compared with the rotational speeds of the pinch-wheel and drive spindle. The drive spindle, being of much lesser diameter than the pinch wheel, rotates much faster. If the wow is of the same speed as the pinch wheel rotation, spin the wheel by hand to see if it is stiff. Dry bearings can cause wow, and a drop of thin oil should put matters right. A sticky deposit on the rubber can also give rise to wow, so a thorough cleaning should be administered.

If the wow is at the same speed as the drive spindle, the trouble could be due to a deposit of oxide on the surface, or a layer of grease or oil; remove by the application of methylated spirit. Also look for something fouling the flywheel (which would be also expected to produce a rubbing or knocking noise) or worn top or bottom flywheel bearings. A drop of methylated spirit on the top bearing will sometimes temporarily cure the wow and thus identify the cause. Oil should not be applied directly as this will introduce drag and cause slow running. For lubrication, oil may be applied sparingly to the *outside* of the phosphor-bronze bearing bead; it will gradually creep through to the working surfaces in very small quantities.

It is possible that the idler wheel between the motor capstan and the flywheel could produce wow, and if the wow frequency does not measure up with the rotational speed of any of the components so far mentioned, the cover plate may be removed to observe the rotation of the idler wheel and its condition. The rubber can perish, becoming either spongy or very hard. A good test is to press a thumbnail into the rubber; it should be firm yet resilient, regaining its shape as soon as the thumbnail is removed. If the recorder has been left in the 'on' position, the idler wheel will have been under tension against the motor capstan, and a small indentation may have formed in its periphery. This will produce a knocking noise, and it can in most cases be cured merely by allowing the recorder to run at its fastest available speed for about half-an-hour.

### Flutter

Flutter is very often due to a hard pressure pad. Roughing it up with a nail file will effect a cure. Dirt on the heads can also produce flutter under certain conditions. A similar effect is sometimes obtained with some of the cheaper unpolished tapes when run at the slowest speed. These tend to bind or stick against the head face and so the tape proceeds with a succession of jerks, usually too rapid to be individually distinguished. The most common result is a squeak or, more accurately, a squawk emanating from the head, and distorted sound reproduction.

A common fault is striction of tape to guide surface, often aggravated by a build-up of shedded oxide in the angles between the guide barrel and its cap or plinth. Routine cleaning should include attention to the guides.

### Slow Running

Slow running, when it is severe and accompanied by irregularities, is often easier to diagnose and put right than running constantly just below normal speed. It is nearly always due to a perished idler wheel or drive belt, the drive belt being particularly prone, because after a prolonged period under tension it loses its elasticity. As with the idler wheel, it can go hard or spongy. If it has gone hard it can often be restored, if only temporarily, by immersing it in boiling water.

Removing and replacing a drive belt can be simple or very difficult, depending on the make and model. When removing the top plate one may be confronted with two or three belts, one from the motor to the flywheel, one from the flywheel to the take-up turntable, and one from one of the turntables to the revolution counter. The one that supplies the drive to the tape most often needs replacement.

Other causes of slow running include greasy deposits on the friction drive surfaces (the motor capstan, idler wheel rim or belt, and flywheel rim) and these will cause slipping. Cleaning all these with meths will remove any such grease. Additionally, if the slipping clutch felt pads on the take-up or paying-out spool are hard or matted, friction will be increased and possibly cause slowing down. Roughing these up in the same way as for a pressure pad will improve matters.

## Lubrication

Lack of lubrication can slow down the works, but care must be taken. A common fault is to apply the wrong lubricant to the wrong places in too great a quantity. Grease can be used for the bottom flywheel bearing, levers and linkages (although this will have no effect on the running speed) but only a thin machine oil elsewhere. Oiling points are the idler wheel and pinch wheel bearings. The flywheel top bearing should not be oiled directly, needing only a trace on the outside of the phosphor bead. Similarly with the motor, which will slow down with the increased drag if oil is applied; only a special very thin oil should be applied to the bearing phosphor bead.

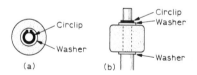

Fig. 13.6 (a) Top view of pinch wheel showing circlip. (b) Side view of pinch wheel assembly.

However, merely oiling is not always sufficient, as the trouble is often due to dirt in the bearings which must be stripped out and cleaned first. In the case of the pinch wheel and idler wheels this is fairly straightforward; a circlip which fits into a groove in the spindle must be prised out, and the wheel can be lifted off. Take care to note the position of various washers and reassemble in the same order. When the wheel is removed, the spindle can be cleaned with meths, as can the inside of the wheel-bush. A touch of thin oil, and refitting, will complete the operation.

Motor bearings sometimes get dirty or clogged with dried-up oil, but dismantling is more involved and it is not recommended for the inexperienced.

**Flywheel Bearing**

The top bearing of the flywheel may get out of line, and is very tricky to get right. It is either bead or thistle shaped, and will line up quite easily when it is loose, but as soon as it is tightened down by means of the clamp plate it tends to move off centre. Unless one is sure that there is something wrong with it, it is best not to disturb it. If it has to be moved, the best way of centring up afterwards is to stand the recorder on end so that the spindle is horizontal. The weight of the flywheel will now be borne partly by the bearing and it should line up in the same plane as the spindle. The clamping screws are then tightened a fraction of a turn each at a time, while simultaneously tapping the end of the spindle to correct any possible movement of the bearing out of true (Fig. 13.7).

When the bearing is tightened, the spindle should be spun and the action of the flywheel should continue the rotation for quite a number of revolutions, depending on its size and weight. It should stop almost imperceptibly, but if the stop can be easily discerned, there is excessive bearing friction and a further attempt at centring must be made. It may take several attempts before friction is reduced to an acceptable level.

Sometimes, the motor itself is at fault and, although the bearings are quite free and clean, it will not develop enough torque to run the recorder at correct speed. Normally the motor will run warm, but if there is a sign of it getting hot, then quite definitely it is faulty and must be replaced. It can be seen from these remarks that slow running can be an elusive fault to trace, and very often professional help must be sought.

**Slow Rewind**

Usually, the rewind starts normally, but will sometimes slow down to a stop as the winding reel fills up and the paying-out reel empties. The reason for this is that the winding reel slows as it fills, thereby decreasing its torque, while the paying-out reel speeds up and back tension friction increases.

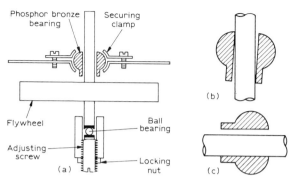

Fig. 13.7 (a) Flywheel assembly showing top of bottom bearing. Top bearing is adjusted by loosening clamp screws. (b) If the top bearing is out of line there will be excessive friction at the top and bottom of the bearing. (c) One way of lining up the top bearing is to lay the recorder on its side, so that the weight of the flywheel along the spindle should bring the bearing into line. The clamp plate can then be carefully tightened in this position.

With single-motor recorders, the trouble is usually due to the clutch friction felt pads hardening, and the cure is to fluff them as previously described. A stretched drive belt will also cause this trouble, but will also affect the normal running speed. With 3-motor machines, the motor itself is often at fault and confirmation should be sought from an engineer. Some slowing with all types of recorder is to be expected near the end of the reel and is acceptable.

## Calling in the Experts

When it becomes necessary to call in expert attention, this does not necessarily imply the local radio shop. Tape recorders need specialist attention and engineers working mainly on radio and television, although technically qualified to attend to tape recorder repairs, may have little practical experience and the familiarity which comes from continually working with them. The recorder should be taken to a firm that either specialises in tape recorders or has a number on sale, indicating that they are conversant with them.

Servicing facilities at the large multiple stores are not usually as good as a well-established reputable smaller concern, as service takes a very secondary position to sales, whereas the reputation of the independent dealer is often built up on service. There are, of course, exceptions to both these rules. It should also be noted that certain makers of tape recorders have their own service depots which can undertake specialist repairs, overhauls and checks under the best possible conditions.

By attending to the regular simple points of maintenance, and putting right any defects as they arise, the recordist will always have confidence in his tape recorder and will not suffer the disappointment of spending time and energy on a recording only to find it has been spoiled by a technical defect in the recorder.

To conclude this chapter, a word or two about tape storage. Tapes do not need to be kept in any particular position and are not easily damaged by physical means. Heat should be avoided, as the tape material may soften and curl if not stored in a cool dry place. Tapes should be kept in dust-proof containers such as the boxes they were packed in. Do not keep them lying around unboxed for extended periods.

Stray magnetic fields can cause partial erasure, so the tape must be kept away from magnets, loudspeakers, power transformers and electric motors. A few feet separation should be sufficient. Magnetic fields from one layer of tape can affect adjacent layers, thus the signal can be transferred to those layers. This will give rise to echo and pre-echo, especially where loud and quiet passages are adjoining. This transference will take place over a period of time, so if the tape is rewound the chances of an adjacent layer being in exactly the same position as before is slight, hence the possibility of print-through is greatly reduced.

The periodic re-spooling of all one's tapes can be rather a chore, especially as the collection grows, but it could be done to a timetable, say a few tapes every couple of months, completely re-spooling in a year—ready to start again! Double-play or triple-play tapes are far more vulnerable to print-through and need to be re-spooled more often than standard-play tapes.

Readers who are technically inclined are referred to *Tape Recorders* by H. W. Hellyer, also published by Fountain Press, which contains detailed sections on the mechanical aspects of the deck, notes on servicing and tests and measurements, together with a great deal of information of value to those with technical experience.

# CHAPTER FOURTEEN

# FURTHER THOUGHTS

IN THE PREVIOUS CHAPTERS we have discussed the major divisions of the creative recording art, each having considerable scope for original and interesting work. One could specialise in only one of these activities and not exhaust the creative possibilities. Even so, there are many further uses of the recorder which have not been mentioned because they are not strictly speaking creative.

## Recording Bird Songs

Bird song recording is not creative on the part of the recordist (other than the creation of a collection of bird songs) but it is a branch of recording requiring skill and patience. The main requirements are a knowledge of ornithology, the birds, their cries, their habitats, and an all-weather outfit of clothing! The principal technical requirement is a portable battery recorder, but the serious recordist will not find a run-of-the-mill machine suitable.

Bird songs contain very high frequencies, some beyond the range of human hearing. To capture the full effect of these demands a recorder and microphone with an extended high-frequency response, without major peaks which would introduce harshness into the recording and destroy the beauty. It may be decided later to do some research on the sounds themselves, perhaps analysing the frequency content and form. Such a project would be seriously hampered by inferior recordings.

Suitable portable recorders are expensive and the potential bird song recordist may have to obtain a second-hand machine (see Chapter 4) or make do with a lesser instrument. In this case look for one with the minimum of frills but which has a good upper frequency response and speed constancy. A multi-speed machine is useful as the highest speed can be used to obtain better frequency response. On the other hand, some quite commendable results have been obtained using a good quality modern cassette recorder, although the convenience of handling will be at the sacrifice of quality.

A directional microphone of the barrel or reflector type should be used. The latter is the most sensitive because it has a large sound-collecting area. It is also cheap and can be used in conjunction with almost any normal microphone of the stick type. However, it is rather bulky and could possibly frighten the quarry unless camouflaged. A stand which enables the microphone to be angled in any direction is also a useful accessory.

Some bird songs may sound rather thin and featureless to our ears because of the large number of harmonics that are near the limit, or out of the range, of human hearing, so we hear only the fundamental frequency and perhaps a few harmonics. Playing recordings of these at lower speeds often reveal unexpected beauties, as the harmonics are brought within normal hearing range. This can be quite an exciting feature of bird-song recording. If there is a local bird-watchers society, it may be worth joining, as they would have accumulated knowledge of local habitats, and may have access to private land where rarer birds find sanctuary.

## Documentaries

The documentary sets out to present a factual account of the chosen subject. It could be the work of an organisation, a tour round a local industry, a day in the life of an individual such as a family doctor, and so forth. Local legend or history can also provide subjects for documentaries.

The main requirement is for the subject to be interesting, not just well produced and planned, although a potentially interesting subject can be spoiled by heavy and unimaginative handling. Presenting an everyday subject in a vivid and absorbing manner is mastery of the art! Always be on the look-out for interesting subjects, those with an unusual aspect or connection, or those capable of interesting development.

Having chosen the subject, detailed research is the next step. Look up and read up all you can find on the subject, and discuss the matter with those involved, obtaining at the same time their permission to proceed with the documentary. Next, a prototype sequence can be worked out with connectives. For example, in the case of a local industry, tracing the product through its successive stages of manufacture would be the obvious sequence. However, it would dull and unimaginative to simply state each time, '*next the product goes to the such-and-such department . . .*'

A variety of different connectives would be needed to keep it interesting. Attention could be drawn to the noise of one department, where machinery is being used, to the comparative quiet of another,

Fig. 14.1   Bird song recording. The parabolic reflector has a built-in microphone with sound insulated cone designed by the author to cut down nearby noise.

where the article may be hand-painted. A description of the unfinished product could be given, followed by the voice of an employee describing what he or she is doing to obtain the final finish. Remember that it is in the presentation and connectives that the creative aspects of this type of recording comes in.

A narrator will usually be necessary to introduce, explain and connect, but use him as sparingly as possible and allow the sounds and voices of the people involved tell most of the story. It is better to have the voice of the operative explaining his job, together with the sounds of the process, than have the narrator describe the action. He can prompt and ask questions, these being edited out later if required as in the case of the interview.

Unlike the interviewee, where hesitation and minor slips can be retained to add atmosphere and spontaneity, the narrator is not really part of the action; he is merely an observer filling in necessary information that cannot be conveyed otherwise. Therefore his narration should be clear, accurate, and precise. The narration should be well scripted in advance to convey the most information with the minimum of words; long-winded rambling explanations are tedious to listen to and will soon kill the interest of the audience. The narration does not have to be recorded in advance or even at the time of the main recording; it is usually preferable to do it afterwards, so that any additional point which may have come up unplanned can be incorporated.

The narrator should have a pleasing voice, or at least one that suits the subject; a piece dealing with education would need a more cultured voice than one, say, on mountaineering. There could be some subjects more appropriate to a female narrator and some even for a well-spoken child. It may be necessary to script a fictional scene to illustrate some part of the documentary. In the case of a day in the doctor's life, one could not record an actual consultation but a typical example could be worked out and acted. Really, the documentary is a combination of many types of recording; interviews, drama, sound sequence and effects, and even background music, which is one reason why discussion of it was left to this final chapter. As with all such recordings, editing can make or mar the final outcome.

## End Notes

There is a very much wider field of creative tape recording work than may at first have been thought possible. In fact, once started, it could be quite a problem to decide what to try. Some activities may have instant appeal and others may not seem to be so interesting. It is a good idea to try several spheres as this will provide experience which will always be useful and may lead to the discovery of an unexpected flair. Having sampled the various forms one may decide to specialise while still retaining a general interest in other areas of activity.

Some recordings may be of outstanding interest, with frequent requests made for their playing. For convenience, these could be transferred to disc so that they may be played in homes which have a record player but no tape recorder. Long-playing records of 7-, 10-, or 12-inch diameter can be cut from the tape by firms specialising in this work and advertising in the tape recording magazines. When sending a tape for a disc to be made, it is always prudent to make a copy first in case the original gets lost in transit.

Many areas have thriving tape clubs where hints are exchanged, demonstrations and lectures arranged, co-operative recording projects devised, and other recording activities arranged. The creative recordist will find membership of such a club helpful to his activities. On a national level there is the Federation of British Tape Recordists and Clubs. Local clubs or individuals can join for a small annual subscription and enrolment fee. Various facilities are offered, including a Sound Archives from which copies can be made for a small fee, and a quarterly magazine *'News and Views'*. Enquiries are welcomed c/o Hon. Secretary 32 Windmill Lane, Southall, Middlesex.

Each year there is a British Amateur Tape Recording Contest open to anyone other than professional recordists. Entries are in various classes: speech and drama, documentary, music, reportage, technical experiment, schools and sounds from nature. Prizes and trophies are awarded for each section. This certainly gives an incentive to produce some really imaginative creative work. Rules and entry forms are available from FBTRC or direct from British Amateur Tape Recording Contest, c/o The Secretary, 33 Fairlawnes Maldon Rd., Wallington, Surrey.

There are various magazines on tape recording, some such as *Studio Sound* catering mainly for the professional. One of particular value to the amateur is *Sound and Picture Tape Recording*, available from newsagents or by direct subscription from the publishers at 16a Bevis Marks, London, E.C.3. This contains articles both technical and on the creative aspect of recording, equipment reviews, and a readers' query answering service, as well as news of tape clubs, new products and developments, and other items of interest. Articles are specially written for the not-too-advanced and there are also contributions from other amateur recordists. In all, a magazine to be recommended.

Whether though one becomes a member of a club or not, whether one uses elaborate and expensive equipment or not, or whether one records in mono, stereo or quad, tape recording affords wide scope for inventiveness and imagination. It can be an interesting hobby, or it can become a serious creative art-form. It is sincerely hoped that this book has given some practical assistance and also stimulated good ideas for creative tape recording.

# INDEX